Sometimes it take... ~~g~~ *...it takes a*

COMMITTEE OF

ONE

Making a Difference,
One Life at a Time

LEILA
WAHBEH

and the
Refugees

PATRICIA MARTIN HOLT

Copyright © 2012 by Patricia Martin Holt

Published by Matriarch Press
Atlanta, Georgia

ISBN: 978-0-9854932-0-2

First Printing

Printed in the United States of America

Cover and Interior Design by GKS Creative

Library of Congress information on file with the publisher

To five of our greatest teachers:
Rama, Buddha, Moses, Jesus, and Mohammed

Chrissy,

Make a difference.

Pat

CONTENTS

Preface   vii

Acknowledgments   xi

1   New Perspectives   1

2   You Don't Cry—You Help   19

3   Don't Teach My People to Beg   25

4   A Bank of Goodness   39

5   We Would Give You Our Blood   47

6   Will You Celebrate?   55

7   It's the Same as if You Put in a Carbon   73

8   I Can Make a Contribution, Can't I?   83

9   The Helpless Become the Helpful   89

10   What Else is There to Do But Learn?   97

11   Who Will Help?   105

12   If You Learn to Count One, Two,
     You Will Reach A Million   113

13   Home Again—1985   119

Photos   127

Epilogue   145

Appendix A: *The Jordan Times* feature article
          about Leila Wahbeh   155

Appendix B: What IS the United Nations Relief
          and Works Agency for Palestine Refugees
          in the Near East?   159

Appendix C: UNRWA Statistics on Camps We Visited
          –Jordan Field Office   161

Bibliography   163

Notes   167

PREFACE

The Middle East had never been part of my plans. I had raised three children while continuing my career consulting to the professions and expected to continue to live well, to vacation in the United States, and to travel abroad only when I could no longer totter to my office.

Then, in December of 1982, I remarried. Our honeymoon included Amman, the capital of Jordan, a small country bounded by Israel, Syria, Iraq, and Saudi Arabia, where my husband, a retired U.S. Geological Survey hydrologist, was working on a water resources consulting assignment. We spent three weeks in a charming Egyptian-owned hotel near the American Embassy, and then moved to an apartment hotel, where I could cook and we could entertain a bit more comfortably.

It was inevitable that I would seek diversion while Lee was working. With my children grown and my career now behind me, time would pass very slowly unless I found new ways to spend it. Thinking that one way I could learn about the country would be to expand my interest in the arts, I began exploring the city's galleries and shops and was astonished by the richness, variety, and quality of the arts and crafts.

Arab women, like Native American women, enhance the browns and beiges of their desert surroundings by looming rugs, weaving tents from goat hair, and plaiting colorful mats from dyed straw. They cross-stitch their floor and throw pillows in blazing colors, as well as their long dresses, with stories of their villages and traditions. Popular with Arab women since the Crusades, counted cross-stitch was only just becoming popular in the States when I left. The dresses, once used for special occasions, have risen to a new level of importance: Palestinian women have been using them as political symbols to declare their heritage.

At a charity showing of Mrs. Widad Kawar's fabulous private collection of traditional Palestinian costumes, I discovered that each village is easily identified by the color and type of fabric used as well as by the choice of motifs displayed in the needlework. My appetite for learning more was whetted, so with Yedida Stillman's invaluable guidebook to the region's embroidery tucked under my arm, I decided to seek one outstanding example of traditional work from Hebron, Ramallah, Bethlehem, and Jerusalem, the crossroads of religion for Jews, Christians, and Muslims. These gathering places created opportunities to see and learn the most sophisticated embroidery techniques. As my knowledge expanded, I would branch out further.

Learning to recognize the designs was difficult but rewarding, part of my reward being the encouragement I got from women who patiently answered my endless questions, and the relationships we established because of my interest in their folklore.

I looked for a piece from Jerusalem first, but was disappointed to learn that it had never developed its own special style. Situated midway between Ramallah and Bethlehem, Jerusalem borrowed designs from both cities and imitated the Bethlehem embroidery and cut. The Jerusalem "style" could only be detected by the fabric, a cotton sateen woven in Aleppo, Syria.

Bethlehem had long been a weaving center, its embroidery famous throughout all of central and southern Palestine. The overall effect is one of color and metallic brilliance and is easily recognizable by its couching[1] in gold metallic thread. This special stitch was used by the Turks and dates at least as far back as the Byzantine period. To have a Bethlehem dress was the dream of every bride, and the lucky ones were handed down embroidered panels carefully saved by their grandmothers and then their mothers from dresses that had long since worn away. Populated mainly by Christian Arabs, the Bethlehem style often incorporates the sign of the cross. Nineteenth-century ceremonial dresses were made of plain stripes of red and green handwoven silk with a yellow silk stripe on the sleeves, until the 1850s, when indigo cotton and orange stripes were introduced.[2]

The embroidery of Hebron is similar to Ramallah's in that red is the predominant color, with touches of green, blue, orange, pink, and brown applied to add interest. Most of Hebron's designs are used elsewhere, but are called by different names. What is called "moon with feathers" in Ramallah is known as "the pasha's tent" in Hebron.[3]

There was a price for such beauty, however. New embroidered dresses, using synthetic fabrics and more recently introduced colors and motifs, cost about 150 dinars (then roughly 450 dollars), and old ones in good condition, now collectors' items, were very expensive. Even small panels rescued from old, worn-out dresses were costly. Less expensive were small pillow covers made from traditional fabrics that, without the use of canvas, hoop, or pattern, replicated the colors and designs of heirloom pieces.

Thus, discouraged by the high cost of the items in the shops, I began to look for ways to meet and deal with the artists directly. The search was most frustrating. New American friends on assignment in Amman took me to the few Arab women who made a business of selling cross-stitched items out of their homes, but, naturally, they were reluctant to reveal their sources as it would cut them out of the small profit that supported their families. When I finally learned that the best work was being done in the refugee camps, I would tell people I met at various functions that I wished to go there, but they would recoil in shock and say they had never visited a camp, didn't intend to, and couldn't imagine why I would be interested in doing so. Didn't I know that the people in the camps disliked Americans? Didn't I know that I might place myself in danger by visiting them? And anyway, who would take me?

But shortly before we were to leave Jordan, a new friend, Vivian Daher, who made her permanent home in Amman, told me she knew someone who might lead me to the sources of the handiwork I so admired. And so, finally, I met Leila Wahbeh. Leila agreed to take me to the artists, to show me their work, and to translate my questions and requests. She told me that the refugees who lived in the camps outside Amman and throughout the entire Middle East were Palestinians who had lost their homes and lands during the 1948 and 1967 wars with Israel. Refugee camps, I thought, were places where people who fled their countries during war or catastrophe gathered together temporarily to be processed so they could join relatives elsewhere until it was safe to return home. How wrong I was.

There was nothing temporary about the situation of the people I met through Leila. Many of them had lived in camps for over forty years, the women keeping alive their hope of returning to their country by continuing, in cloth, the stories of their lives, their heritage, and their traditions.

As I grew to know Leila, my admiration for the needlework expanded to include admiration for a woman whose inner beauty is as rich and brilliant as the work done by her people. Strong, dedicated, and purposeful, Leila's days are spent building bridges of happiness and living her motto: In order to achieve, we must first survive.

Let me tell you about Leila. Our conversations and the stories told by the Palestinian refugees were recorded by me as they were being translated from Arabic. Only after reading about Leila and about some of the people whose dignity she has helped to recover, will you, too, understand what can be accomplished—anywhere—by a *Committee of One*.

ACKNOWLEDGMENTS

The kindness and generosity shown to me by so many in Amman has continued since my return home. Special thanks to Miriam Abulaban; Karen Asfour; Rosemary Bdier; Vivian Daher; Mary Lou Harwood; Kirsten Lowzow; Mary Mufti; Ed and Salwa Nassar; Ivy Nasir; Edward, Niki, and Lina Qungar; Ann Sawalha; and Ilse, Naji, and Melina Tannous. The journey from pen to publisher was made smoother by Elizabeth Fernea, author and senior lecturer at the Center for Middle Eastern Studies at the University of Texas at Austin, who read my manuscript and suggested I send it to Grace Halsell, journalist and author of several well-known books on the Middle East. It was Ms. Halsell who guided me to editor Doris Safie, whose patience and skill brought this project to fruition.

My deepest gratitude to my dear daughters, Leann Phenix, who guided me to the Cadence Group, and Gerryll Gae Hall, whose faith in this project never wavered, to my granddaughter Melissa Kelley for her endless patience, to Devens Gust for believing in me from the beginning, and to the friends whose interest in this project has remained steadfast through every twist and turn in the journey—Cecilia Benites, Lynn Sanders, Marjorie and Bernie Combs, John and Naomi Fucik, Catherine Gourley, Susan Williams, the Joseph Najjar family, especially my Lara, and Diane Hawkins-Cox—and to the warm and gracious people in the refugee camps who shared their stories with me.

CHAPTER ONE

New Perspectives

VIVIAN PHONED ME A FEW WEEKS BEFORE we were to leave Amman and said I could accompany her and Leila to the Souf Refugee Camp the next morning. I was told to dress conservatively, to wear a scarf over my hair, and once inside the camp, to do exactly as I was instructed. I was waiting outside on the curb when they drove up, and both women got out to greet me. As we shook hands after Vivian's introduction, I looked into Leila's smoky brown eyes, wise and lovely, and was immediately drawn to her. Although Vivian was wearing Western dress like me, Leila wore a traditional long black dress, heavily cross-stitched at the bodice and hem. I asked Leila if I, as a first-time visitor, had dressed appropriately.

"Oh, yes. Everyone will know you are a foreigner. This is my dress for every occasion. I wear it to identify with my people." I smiled in relief and climbed into the back seat of her little car.

"Vivian has told me about you, Pat," Leila continued as we pulled away. "When the meanings of the designs are explained to you, you will have a great appreciation for our art."

Then she and Vivian talked about an upcoming bazaar at the

American School, where Vivian is the librarian. Her contacts through the school and the foreign community in Amman assist her in promoting the sale of Palestinian women's cross-stitched articles; hence her initial connection to Leila.

I sat back expecting to enjoy the ride, but soon learned that when Leila drove, relaxation was not to be part of the trip. A narrow two-lane highway winds to Souf Camp, outside the city of Jerash, about fifty kilometers north of Amman. To get there, a driver simply goes as fast as traffic will allow, passes on curves and hills, and uses the horn as a warning signal. I gazed determinedly out the side window, praying that Leila would concentrate more on driving than talking.

The March air was crisp, and the skies a bright, clear blue. From time to time, I spotted the gray goat-hair tents used by the Bedouin. Shepherds guarded large flocks of sheep on the stark and rocky hillsides. Goats seemed to herd themselves until children scampered from behind boulders, their switches moving the flocks along as they grazed. We passed a young girl standing in a stream. She held the bridle of her burro with one hand, and filled the large leather water bags it carried with the other. The full bags appeared to weigh as much as the tiny animal.

The car slowed to a crawl to avoid hitting pedestrians. We passed a high chain-link fence on our right and cement block structures on our left. Boys were hanging by their fingertips from the fence or racing toward it, and from somewhere in the vicinity I heard a sound new to my ears, a shrill high-pitched *lalalala*. It was the camp's communications network sounding the alert, Vivian explained. "Umm Zaki's here!" Other voices shouted, "Umm Zaki! Umm Zaki!"

By the time we stopped, women were coming from doorways all around us. Leila signaled a sharp right turn with her horn, moved onto a narrow, muddy pathway, then slowed to stop. I had my first glimpse of refugee living.

The cement block–attached houses were the size of one small room, perhaps 3x4 meters, with cement floors and corrugated tin roofs. All were doorless, facing tiny enclosed courtyards where the cooking was done. Most had no windows. After we passed the schoolyard fence, there were no more roadsides. The courtyard gates abutted the edge of the roadway. Pedestrian traffic was so dense that Leila drove very slowly, with one hand on the horn. When people turned to see who was honking, their faces lit up and smiles flashed from every direction.

"Everyone knows you, Leila," I exclaimed.

"I spend much time here. We must help these poor people."

We stopped then. "Come, you will meet one of the ladies who makes the pillow covers." Vivian got out of the car.

"Pat, they are leery of foreigners here. Your red hair is very noticeable. Cover all of it, and take off your shoes when you are invited to enter."

Had the network reached this far? A small, worn, barefoot woman, wearing a long dress and a scarf over her hair, came from her doorway, arms outstretched, smiling and welcoming, "Marhaba, Umm Zaki." She also recognized Vivian and took her hand. When Leila spoke with her, she gestured to me to follow into her house. We all removed our shoes.

The house was pathetically bare. There were no cupboards or furniture. Several thin mattresses were stacked on one side of the room. On the other side were shelves made from cardboard boxes that contained dishes and clothing. The lower portion of the walls had been painted a vivid aqua, with a splattering of white polka dots. Spread out on the bare floor before us were a dozen or so completed pillow fronts, containing thousands of tiny stitches. Every hole in the canvases had been filled with brilliant colors and glorious designs. We sat on one of the mattresses pulled down for us so Leila could inspect the work closely. The woman asked for approval of her work by handing each one to Leila expectantly, waiting to hear *kwayyis,* meaning "good."

We didn't want to distract Leila, so Vivian leaned close to me so we could talk quietly. "Umm Ruz has been working to complete these covers since Leila's last visit when she brought the threads and canvases. Leila will take these fronts to another woman in Amman who will finish them. After the bazaar, Leila will deduct the cost of material and thread and will use the rest to buy food, fuel, and medicine for Umm Ruz and the finisher."

"When is the bazaar?" I asked.

"Oh, in a few months," she answered offhandedly.

"But there's no light in here. It's freezing cold, and this woman is barefoot! We can see our breath, for God's sake! How can she sew under these conditions?" Leila's glance indicated my whispers had escalated. When she continued her conversation with Umm Ruz, Vivian resumed the story.

"She sits in the doorway during the daylight hours and works as long as she can. She has to support her children."

"Children? You mean children live here, too?"

"She has six children. They attend UNRWA schools here in the camp. We passed one when we entered. None of her children is old enough to support the family. Her husband is dead. She is raising them from the sewing that Leila obtains for her."

"Vivian, I have some money with me. Please take it. She needs fuel oil now, not in July." I reached for my purse.

"I can't take it. Money never changes hands. Leila knows what each family needs. She has kerosene and rice and bread for this woman in the trunk of her car, but she will not give money. It is against her principles."

Leila rose, her business concluded. She took most of the covers with her, leaving only two to be improved. The woman accompanied us to the car to help remove bags of groceries and more thread and canvases. She hugged Leila, smiling, and shook our hands good-bye.

As soon as the car doors closed, my questions started. "Leila, why do they call you Umm Zaki? Why not Leila?"

"A Muslim woman becomes *Umm* or 'mother of,' followed by the name of her first child, and a man becomes *Abu* or 'father of,' followed by the name of the first child. So each parent has two names. I am Leila and Umm Zaki. My husband is Yahya and Abu Zaki. If the first child is a girl, you are Umm and her name until a boy is born. Then you take his name. It is the name of the oldest son that is important."

"I see. Vivian said the children go to UNRWA schools. What's that?" I moved to the edge of my seat to hear better.

Vivian answered. "UNRWA stands for United Nations Relief and Works Agency for Palestine Refugees in the Near East. It is responsible, through donations by member nations and private giving, for providing basic services to about 2 million registered refugees who live in camps all over the Middle East. There are ten camps here in Jordan."

"Who qualifies to be registered?"

"Anyone who lived in Palestine for at least two years before the 1948 War with Israel and who lost both his home and livelihood as a result of the war. To receive UNRWA aid, he has to register and be in need, and have taken refuge on the West Bank, in Jordan, Lebanon, the Syrian Arab Republic, or the Gaza Strip. In 1948, there were only about three-quarters of a million Arabs in camps. Now the population has almost doubled, and their descendants, if they qualify, also receive assistance."

"You mean all these people lived in Palestine and had to leave when Israel was declared a state?"

"As a result of that war and the 1967 War, yes."

"What kind of assistance do the refugees receive?"

"Education and health and sanitation services. Extreme hardship cases receive shelter and some food," Vivian replied. "Pat, this is a very sensitive issue. As a result of visiting the camps and seeing the realities of daily living, we are not the people to talk to about the assistance provided. If you really want to understand UNRWA's part in assisting the people,

I suggest you stop by their office in Amman. It is important that you understand their role accurately from the outset if you are going to spend much time here."

I changed the subject. "How old is Umm Ruz?"

"She is thirty-two," Leila answered, after calculating a little.

"She looks closer to fifty!"

"This is a hard life. There have been many sorrows for these women. And no end seems to be coming."

Thirty-two, I thought. That was only a little older than my eldest daughter, soon to graduate with a degree in veterinary medicine, with her whole life before her. Umm Ruz had looked so tired. So old. Yet her face had shone with pride when Leila complimented her. What a brave soul she was, to create art of infinite beauty and variety in the midst of this gray and stultifying misery.

I asked one last question. "Leila, is there some meaning in the way Umm Ruz used the paint in her house?"

"Yes, Pat." There was the slightest edge to Leila's voice. "Umm Ruz sits on the floor to do her work. She was trying to brighten the lower part of the room, what she sees and where she props up the pillows to rest her back during the day. She used white to add a little interest, but she ran out of paint before she could finish."

Her answer silenced me. There was so much to learn about the plight and the pride of the refugees.

We pulled up at another gate. A rickety fence surrounded two small buildings. As we entered, I observed that one was used as a kitchen/storeroom, and the other, where we sat, was the living room/bedroom. The cooking was done outdoors over an open fire. Seven women had assembled, their several children with them. Shoes were again removed, scarves donned, mattresses put down. We sat with our backs against the wall, our legs tucked under us. (It is an insult to show the bottoms of your feet to anyone.) Leila began talking with the women, while I tried to follow the conversation. A project was obviously under way: boxes of embroidery floss were brought out and threads selected; material was examined for flaws and measured from nose-to-arm length.

In the midst of this busy camaraderie, one woman left the group and returned with a tray of food that she placed on the floor in the center of the group. I watched the women dip thin Arab bread in oil and then into a green powder before eating it. There were also hot hard-boiled, eggs, sliced tomatoes, sweet coffee, and tea. The women urged me to help myself with their eyes and gestures. I hesitated, knowing how desperately they needed the food themselves, but when Vivian and Leila told me the women would be highly insulted if I did not partake, I helped myself to an egg—something I recognized. There was more urging.

"What is the green powder?" I asked Vivian. Leila was always busy speaking Arabic with everyone, and I didn't want to interrupt her.

"It is thyme, called *za'atar* in Arabic. Very good for your digestion. You must eat. Come."

I smiled gamely at all the watching eyes, had a little of everything, all of it tasty, and made a mental note to serve bread with za'atar and oil to my husband, who was always interested in what I learned on my daily forays.

After lunch, Leila finished her instructions to the ladies, and they prepared a package of completed items for her to take home. We bid cheerful good-byes and headed for the next stop, which Leila explained would be Baqa'a Camp. Lying in a fertile valley, this camp is only twenty minutes outside Amman. During the drive, Leila told me the women were making a long dress of traditional fabric and design for one of her daughters and items for the same bazaar I had overheard her and Vivian discuss on our way to Souf that morning.

Then she said, "We are stopping at Baqa'a so I can show you the school library I am building."

"You're building a library? For how many students?"

"Twenty-five hundred girls. There are so many, they must go in two shifts."

Imagine being able to say, offhandedly, that you were building a library for 2,500 children. I pictured it in my mind's eye. Rows and rows of books to teach the children about the world outside the camp, inviting them to become a part of that world, inspiring them to leave this squalor.

"I have been told," I said, "that the Palestinians in the camps believe all Americans are their enemy because our government supports Israel. Since coming here, I have grown resentful of the narrowness of my education, with its emphasis on the West. Will these children be taught both sides of this issue, so they can come to their own conclusions?"

"What is conclusions?" Leila replied, impatient with my English word.

"To make up their own minds."

"What is to make up? These people were removed from their lands. All they want is to go home in peace. That is all. The children must not forget their heritage. We will stir their hearts to remember Palestine. They must learn about their country and the world."

We turned into Baqa'a Camp. All I'd seen that morning was repeated. The narrow, rutted streets, the sewage flowing down shallow trenches in the middle of every roadway, the teeming humanity. Disaster films flashed through my mind—houses falling to pieces, and endless streams of half-clothed people running through the streets, with expressions of bewilderment. It couldn't be happening, their expressions said. Yet here they were, and it was.

"How many people live here, Leila?"

"About 100,000."

"On how much land?" It seemed so cramped. The attached houses were clustered almost on top of each other.

"About 1,400 dunums." (The equivalent of 350 acres, one dunam is 1,000 square meters, 0.2471 acre, approximately 4 dunams to an acre..)

"When was it started?"

"After the 1967 War. So was Souf Camp, which is smaller. There, only about 15,000 people live on 500 dunums."

When we reached the school, hundreds of girls surrounded the car shouting for Umm Zaki. The principal, buttoned up in a drab floor-length coat, with a scarf over her hair, met us in the doorway. Vivian whispered, "Strict Muslim women allow only members of their family to see them with their hair uncovered or their arms and legs bare."

The principal returned to her desk, a poorly made table covered with oilcloth. Several sagging shelves next to the door contained papers that appeared to be homework or loose sheets belonging to the teachers. Otherwise, the room was bare. There was no telephone, no carpet, no file cabinet, nothing to indicate her status. After greeting us warmly in English, she gave Leila the key to the library. The building stood next to her office. Again, the cement blocks, the cement floor, the holes waiting for windows. The room was rectangular and about the size of three of the rooms we had just visited. Four bare lightbulbs hung from the ceiling. Against the back wall were shelves constructed of poor quality plywood. A counter of the same material limited access to the shelves, which contained twenty-six books for 2,500 students. Twenty-six books. Leila saw my dismay.

"It is a beginning. We have donations of English books. The children need Arabic books. They are not easy to get. We have no paper. The government has started a tree-growing project. Someday we will have forests. Now, it isn't easy. When the children finish their lesson books, they must erase all the marks and reuse the paper. There is no money for more. Paper is very expensive."

The principal then joined us for a while. After a few words with her, we said good-bye.

I could see that Leila wasted no time, a woman after my own heart. I asked her what her visit had accomplished.

"Today was to see the progress. The windows must be donated and delivered. We want to plant trees outside. The people will use this room as a social center as well. We must get tables and chairs. So I see what they need and get it."

On our way to the next visit, Leila stopped the car in the middle of the road as it became apparent that the car would get stuck if we continued on it. We got out, and as Vivian and I slipped and slid in and out of the icy ruts, clutching each other to keep from falling, Leila strode confidently ahead, knowing just where to step through the maze of byways. As we made our way, Leila told us about Ahmad, a young paralyzed man.

"I am working to get him a little carpentry shop, but it is a problem. We found a hut near him that he could use for a shop, but the street is so bad, Ahmad can't roll his wheelchair from his house down to the shop. Also we have no tools yet, and no wood. So first we must get the street fixed so he can get to his work."

"Who fixes the streets?"

"UNRWA is supposed to fix them. They are in charge of maintaining streets, garbage pickup, sewage, all things to keep the people healthy."

"Then why is sewage running down the middle of these streets?"

"UNRWA is limited by the donations it receives. So I get donations of cement and—what you call black?"

"Asphalt."

"Yes, and things to repair the streets."

At the gate to Ahmad's house, Leila knocked sharply. A young woman shyly peeked out, then, recognizing Leila, beamed as she opened the gate wide, allowing us to enter. Immediately inside, tied with a string to the gatepost, was a baby goat. Sitting on the ground next to it, in a crudely built wire cage, was a dove. I found it odd; not one home that I visited in

Amman had a pet in evidence, yet here was a family with two of them. The doorways to the small structure were only a few feet from the gate. The young woman went through one, and we went through the other.

A thin young man with brown hair lay on a single bed, facing the wall. A worn blanket covered the sheets. When he heard Leila's voice, he turned over and stretched out his hand to her and Vivian. I looked around the unheated room at the unpainted cement block walls, the tin roof, and the bare cement floor. A wheelchair and a small table next to the bed completed the furnishings. Over Ahmad's bed hung a large black-and-white photo of Queen Alia, who died (tragically young) in a helicopter crash south of Amman in 1977.

After the three of them had talked for a few minutes, Vivian spoke with him alone. I asked Leila what had happened, but Ahmad answered me. He had understood my question. I flushed with embarrassment.

"It is all right. Umm Zaki has made it all right. I will tell you what happened."

"Please tell me, Ahmad. I am ashamed. I should have asked you if you could speak English."

"I am thirty-three years old. My family is originally from the village of Jimzo, located in the Lydda District in Palestine. When they were driven from Jimzo in the 1948 War, they found refuge in the Gaza Strip, which at that time was occupied by the Egyptian Army. My father, an auto mechanic, joined the Egyptian government workshops in Gaza. He met and married my mother in 1950. I was born in 1954.

"By 1967 there were seven of us, two boys and five girls. After the 1967 War, Israel forced people across the Allenby Bridge to the East Bank. My family crossed with the crowds to Baqa'a Camp. My father preferred to continue to work in the workshops. They had been reestablished in Cairo, so he married an Egyptian woman and took me to live with them there. My mother settled here in Baqa'a as a permanent refugee. She depended partially on UNRWA food rations and partially on some money from my father, who never divorced her. It was too little to take care of all of the children, so she got a job cleaning government offices. Despite her hard work and the money my father sent her, there was not enough to educate my brother or my sisters, all of whom married after a primary education. I successfully completed my studies, enrolled at the Art Institute, and graduated in 1974 with a degree in Painting, Art, and Publicity.

"In vain I tried to find a job. Ultimately, I went to Iraq, hoping for a better chance to work. Unfortunately, I was hurt in a car accident. My spine was broken. I was left in a fetal position, paralyzed. I was first hospitalized in Baghdad Hospital for four months, until November of 1976, and was then transferred to Hussein Medical Center in Amman. I remained there in physical therapy until March of 1977, with little improvement. After the long course of treatment, I settled here in Baqa'a with my mother.

"Quite bedridden, I was sad and depressed. My mother, our symbol of devotion and filial piety, went blind as a complication of her diabetes. My sister's hands are crippled by arthritis. She carried my mother on her back to the water closet and washed our clothes with her feet. This aggravated my condition. I felt so helpless. My family had counted on me, on my education, to take away our misfortunes and to change our future. Now my mother had no husband, no sight, and no help from her only educated son. I became subject to repeated attacks of agonizing pain, and decided life was unbearable. I tried to kill myself by taking a whole bottle of sedatives. Unfortunately, at least so I thought then, I was discovered, and the emergency unit saved me.

"Some time later, neighbors reported my condition to Umm Zaki, who visited me. It was she who arranged for me to be seen free of charge at the Hussein Medical Center. It was she who arranged an operation at no cost so that I can now sit upright. The doctors also removed the kidney stones that had caused me such great pain and so many attacks. It was Umm Zaki who found a donor to supply me with this wheelchair. The settlement didn't come for a long time after the accident. When I received it, she obtained this small lot in my name. Then she recruited materials for this residence and my little shop with capital donated by a benevolent society.

"My mother is now sixty years old. She is supported by my brother who works in agriculture in the Jordan Valley.

"Last year, my father, who was frail and chronically ill with gastric trouble, died in Cairo from a heart attack. He was only fifty-six.

"As yet I've been unable to get a car for the handicapped, so it is difficult to drive to Amman to obtain employment at a newspaper office. That is why we've set up this little shop. We talked about what I could do to support myself and decided that perhaps I can learn carpentry. I have hope Umm Zaki will find a way for me to begin."

The timing couldn't have been better. It was almost eerie that I had been introduced to him.

"Thank you, Ahmad, for sharing your story with me. I can see why Leila would be eager to help you. You're a courageous young man." I looked at Leila. "Would it be acceptable for me to offer an idea? Ahmad may be the perfect person to implement it."

A warning emanated from Leila. Her look said I wasn't to hurt this man. I wasn't to offer him false hope.

"An American friend left Amman a few weeks ago. He took with him for his family and friends several pairs of small wooden dolls he bought from a local shop. There are no moving parts, just a small head with a face and head covering painted on it, and a body with a traditional costume, arms, and hands painted on it. It is shaped somewhat like a clothespin. The dolls were so well-received that he wrote to ask me to find someone here to produce them for his wife's gift shop."

"Draw one for us, Pat," Vivian said, digging into her purse. She produced a pencil and paper. "We can find someone to donate the wood cut to the right size."

I drew the doll clumsily. Vivian looked at the sketch, and said, "Oh, Pat, I know which dolls you mean. They are painted and lacquered, and each pair has a man and a woman in a particular village's traditional costume."

"Exactly."

"I have a pair at my house!"

"Then Ahmad shall have a sample," Leila joined in.

Vivian squeezed my arm, saying, "This is an excellent idea."

I could feel the excitement in the room. Ahmad was struggling to sit up. He took the paper from Vivian and examined it closely.

"These are quite small," he said. "It wouldn't take me long to make one."

Leila took Ahmad's hand. "You see, Ahmad. It is as we said. You have survived. And now you will achieve."

It was just like the days of being in business. All kinds of ideas flashed at me.

"May I make another suggestion?" I asked, hesitantly this time. I was afraid of my optimism.

"By all means, by all means," Leila replied.

"Friends and I will gather for you books with color pictures of people in our traditional costumes, such as Pilgrims, cowboys and cowgirls, men and women from different periods of our history, soldiers in the uniforms of various wars, and so on. Ahmad can produce them. They can be sold to tourists here, at bazaars, or at fairs in the States. Vivian can tell you that there are many, many arts and crafts fairs in our country. People will buy small, inexpensive items readily if they are nicely made."

Vivian voiced her agreement. "It is true, Leila. I have seen nothing like these dolls anywhere in the States. Surely there is a way to handle this. We will find it."

Giddy with happiness, we said good-bye to Ahmad.

"I am glad you came to my house. I ask you to please come again," Ahmad said with quiet dignity.

"I will, Ahmad. I thank you for forgiving my curiosity and for telling me about yourself. I will send the pictures to you through Leila." He shook my hand.

"And I will bring the dolls very soon, Ahmad," Vivian answered him.

We went back to the car. "My heart goes out to him," I told Leila. "I pray he will become self-sufficient in this new occupation."

"He is cared for now, which is the main thing. His mother, his brother, and his brother's wife, the young woman you saw, live in the attached room. The wife cooks and cares for Ahmad and his mother."

"What about the pets?"

"Pets?" Leila was puzzled.

"Yes. The goat and the dove. Do they help Ahmad keep up his spirits?"

I was getting into the car. Leila put her hand on mine as it rested on the top of the door. It stopped me.

"Those animals are not pets, Pat. Kind people in the camp have given them to Ahmad for food. The family will eat the bird soon. The kid will provide milk and cheese after a while, and finally meat. No. They are not pets."

I lowered my eyes, forced once again to confront the meaning of utter destitution. As we drove back to Amman, Leila and Vivian wrapped up their plans for the bazaar. I mentally reviewed the day. Ahmad had affected me so. As did the woman with her pillow covers. There must be a way for her and the other widows who were the sole support for their children to continue. Leila told me it took each woman at least eighty hours to make one pillow front, for which she received eight to ten dinars. She couldn't possibly care for children on so little, even without the high rent, utilities, and transportation costs she saved by living at the camp. I interrupted Leila.

"Can you increase the price of the pillows to give the women more money?"

"If they cost too much, no one will buy them. And the women will have no money at all. You wanted to meet the artists to save the cost in the shops."

"That is true, Leila. But I would have no objection to paying the women fifteen dinars, knowing it would go directly to them. The shops are charging twenty dinars or more, and you tell me that the women get half of that or less."

"What can we do? There are few places to sell their items here. Just the bazaars and a few shops." Lips set, she shook her head sadly.

"Can't the daughters help with the work?"

"The girls don't want to learn. They see their mothers working so hard, making their eyes bad, and there is no money. They want to get jobs and leave the camps when they graduate from school to marry or attend college."

"But if the work isn't continued, the art will die. It must be preserved."

"We wish it to be so. You may choose from the pillow covers those you wish to buy. I will see you again so you can decide." She pressed the accelerator and we sped back to Amman.

As we pulled up in front of our apartment hotel, I was struck by the contrast of the two worlds—the modern city and the refugee camp. I was to be in Jordan this time for only a few more weeks before returning to the United States, and yet I could not shake off the images of the women working in the cold over their fabric, of Ahmad struggling to survive, of my own lack of awareness. I got out of the car and looked in at Leila.

"I would like to go back again with you. If there is time. If you think I could."

She flashed a smile, then nodded. As the car drove away, I looked after her, realizing how much I had to learn from Leila, my link to the Palestinian people and to a new perspective on the explosive world that is the Middle East.

Subsequently, Leila told me that a friend had brought Queen Alia's mother to visit Ahmad. Not knowing who she was, Ahmad asked if Queen Alia had helped her and said, "I know if she were alive, she would have helped me." The next day help arrived.

1998 – Umm Ruz has died. Ahmad later obtained a job at a newspaper and left the camp. He is married with three children. One is named after Leila's son Zaki, the other after Queen Alia's son. The children attend university in Egypt.

CHAPTER TWO

You Don't Cry— You Help

I RAN UP THE STAIRS TO OUR APARTMENT WHERE Lee was waiting for me and poured my heart out to him, describing the children, the library, the paralyzed man who couldn't get to his shop and who would have no wood or tools when he did, and last, Umm Ruz, the woman who, with a talent for creating beauty, could not afford to paint her walls. "Lee, they have nothing! Not even shoes in some cases, unless they're donated. The rooms we visited were freezing cold, they have no space to work, yet they create beautiful art. How can we help them? Leila tells me there's very little market for their products here." He handed me a cup of coffee.

"Pat, I feel sorriest for the paralyzed man. The women get needles and threads and materials. He has nothing. Can you imagine how frustrated he must be?"

"I know. What can we do? How can we help?"

"Well, one way would be to sell the goods for the women and send them money. We'd have to find a way to get them to the States through nonprofit organizations, though. Otherwise, customs and duties will leave nothing for them."

"Oh, Lee! That's a perfect idea!" I jumped up from the table and reached over to hug him. He lowered his head, patted my arms, and mumbled something about getting used tools for Ahmad.

A few days before our departure, Leila called to see if I wished to go with her for the day. I was waiting for her when she pulled up. With her was a young French woman in the early stages of pregnancy. She was employed by a Swiss charitable organization that helped the handicapped, and was visiting Amman to find out how the organization could help the refugees. Someone had directed her to Leila. Her hair was plaited in thick, dark braids, and she spoke with an enchanting accent. After my introduction to Monique, Leila asked me my news, and we sped off.

"Leila, we want to try to sell the women's work in the U.S. It must not stop, and if the daughters see money coming in, perhaps they will have the incentive to learn. We see only one problem."

"What is that?"

"Shipping. It must be shipped through nonprofit agencies on each end to save the money from customs and duties."

"It is a good idea, Pat. You must begin to look for a way to receive the goods when you go back to the States."

"Right. I'll buy several items from you to use as samples to show merchants. Perhaps when I come back in the fall, I'll have orders."

It was amazing, I reflected as we drove to Baqa'a. I had known Leila only a little while, and already her energy had propelled me into action. What kind of magic did this woman have to make me respond so quickly and positively? My glimmer of insight became a glow. She assumed the best of everyone. She assumed that once people saw the camps, action would naturally be taken. And it was. She assumed that when she asked for help, it would be given, with no expectation of gratitude or reward. And it was. She assumed that everyone's compassion and generosity matched her own. That was Leila's special magic.

She explained that we would stop briefly at a dental clinic she had just furnished. The dental chair and equipment had been donated and were to be in use when we arrived. Then we could continue on our mission. When we arrived at the clinic, Leila was annoyed that no one was sitting on the bench outside the building awaiting treatment.

The dentist greeted all of us warmly. As he and Leila discussed the equipment, I gazed around the spare little room. Conditions were primitive. The water used to rinse out flowed down into a trench on the floor and out a large hole pounded into the side of the building. The dentist told Leila that a part was missing from a piece of his equipment and that he would need it soon.

"Where are your patients?" Leila asked.

"Everyone is well," the dentist replied.

Leila's eyebrows shot up. "No poor people? No one who needs his teeth made better? How much do you make each month?"

The dentist sensed he had committed an error. Leila was wrathful. She commanded us to come, and we trotted after her as she stormed from the room, muttering in Arabic, and then saying in English, "In Amman I shall report him to UNRWA. He is heartless to ignore these people. In his white jacket with his hands in his pockets doing nothing, he earns 300 dinars a month!"

Leila serene is of medium height; angry she is much taller. She strode to the car, got in, and slammed the door, then drove us to several areas of Baqa'a, showing Monique cases of crippled children and adults who needed braces, wheelchairs, or therapy. Each case was more pitiful than the last. Everywhere we stopped, Leila questioned people to get information about others needing help and directions in finding them.

"One last stop," she said, driving very slowly, "then we will be going home."

As we approached, several women rushed at the car, stopping it abruptly. They had been waiting for a small blue car with foreigners in it. The network had reached them.

All atwitter, the women led us to a gate opening onto a tiny yard of hard-packed earth. A few scrawny chickens scratched frantically for a kernel of food. The women pointed to the doorway of what appeared to be an abandoned, decrepit hut. Leila cautiously peeked inside, then clapped her hand to her mouth, and backed away from the doorway. Monique, concerned at her reaction, rushed to Leila's side. The women moved past them, went in, and carried out a bundle of rags. I held back, afraid, as they unwrapped the bundle to expose a bony, withered old Bedouin woman, sitting with her legs bent Indian fashion. One of the women lifted the old lady's dress, exposing pencil thin legs and horribly deformed knees, the caps of which protruded eight to ten inches above her legs. We were told she hadn't walked for years and depended on the goodness of neighbors to bring her an occasional dish of food and assist her with her bodily functions. The rest of the time she sat alone in the dark hut with nothing, no one. Her sons were dead. I realized, horror-stricken, that this might have been my mother, Lee's mother, any mother, and ran to the car sobbing. Leila came after me and spun me around to face her.

"You don't cry! You help!" Her face was drawn.

"Oh, Leila, I can't stand it! I can't!"

"My tears have filled the sea. There are no more tears. Will your tears make her legs straight? No! Will your tears bring back her dead sons? No! We must solve this problem, that is what we must do. The people have led us here to help this woman. The Swiss agency must help her."

"But, Leila, how does she eat? Who takes care of her?" I tried to muffle my sobs, but it was no use.

She reached into the car for her keys with one hand and took my arm firmly with the other.

"You will help me take her rice and oil and eggs. Come."

Monique was still examining the old woman, who trembled and held her hands to her eyes to keep out the brightness of the day. Leila gave the bags of groceries to the neighbors, translating instructions from Monique to them, and we left.

Conversation on the drive home centered on cases they had seen, what could be done, and when. Monique assured Leila that all she had seen would be reported to her agency with recommendations, and that action would follow. I was too depressed to participate in the talk.

"We are here, Pat. Will I see you before you leave?"

"So we are. I'm sorry. I was preoccupied. No, we won't have another chance to be together until I return."

As we got out of the car, I remembered the pillow covers.

"Oh, Leila, did you bring things for me to use as samples for the merchants?"

She opened the trunk and handed me a package.

"This will give you a variety of pieces of different sizes and prices."

I paid her, saying, "I'll work hard to get orders and will keep in touch with you to let you know when we're coming back. Please, Leila, let me go with you when we return. I promise I'll never cry again where anyone can see me. I promise."

She smiled and we hugged each other goodbye.

The Bedouin woman died a few weeks after our visit.

CHAPTER THREE

Don't Teach My People to Beg

LEILA'S PHONE RANG EARLY ONE COLD JANUARY morning in 1978. Mrs. Sharpee, the French ambassador's wife, and Mrs. Lisa Hamzeh, a British woman married to an Arab doctor, were calling to ask her to come with them to solve a problem that needed immediate attention. Children living at an orphanage in Wadi-al-seer, a small town on the edge of Amman, were stealing food from local shops. Leila, always responsive to any request for help, met them, and they drove together to the town.

What they found were sixty children from three to nine years of age, ill-fed, living by themselves, no one caring for them. There was no glass in the windows, the water had stopped running, and the stove and refrigerator did not work. The house reeked with the smell of clogged toilets and bare mattresses soaked with urine. Many of the children wore nothing but a tattered shirt.

Leila was so outraged that she called a reporter at the local television station to come with his camera. His pictures would make it impossible to protest that such conditions could not exist in Amman. No one would be able to deny the stark misery of these abandoned children.

After families were found to care for the orphans temporarily, she called the Royal Court and asked for an appointment with King Hussein. Had she notified the proper ministry with the results of her investigation (the cook had taken the food and had done no work, and the director was obviously unreliable), she would have been told to write a letter. The situation would have continued until an answer could be formulated. But when King Hussein saw the film on television, he acted quickly by giving strict instructions that the situation be righted immediately. The program, which ran for an hour, ended with requests for donations of food, clothing, housing, and help for the children. The response was tremendous. The Ministry of Social Welfare assisted Leila in creating an Orphans' Society so that donations would be tax deductible. A family rented a large house to the Society as an orphanage. Donations of clothing, beds, food, and other necessities for the house gave them the start they needed.

As a result, the children now live at the orphanage, eat wholesome meals, leave for school each day, and return each night to a clean, healthy, well-staffed environment. The conscientious staff provides the care and love the children had lived without for so long. Leila, a whirlwind of activity, accomplished this monumental task in less than a month.

She was in her forty-third year and had been working with Palestinian refugees for twenty of them. It all started in Jerusalem, when her husband, a pediatrician, told her about the young widows who were forced to leave their small children home alone in order to work at the government hospital where he practiced. He told her how weak, ill, and undernourished the children were and asked her to go to the camp to see for herself. She was to learn to her despair that the Jericho Camp, fifty kilometers outside Jerusalem, typified conditions in all the camps throughout the Middle East. She found thousands of children, barefoot and in rags, playing in the sewage that flowed down the middle of the narrow dirt pathways. Families lived in tents or dark, bare hovels, with little food and few possessions. All had been lost when they fled for their lives from their villages to areas on the West Bank of the Jordan River during the 1948 War with Israel. She was stunned by the squalor and poverty. These people had been the backbone of her country, the farmers and the shepherds. They had been self-sufficient.

When she returned home, she described the appalling conditions to her husband, and they decided together that she must begin on a case-by-case basis to help her people, always seeing for herself, always solving the problems individually. She had undertaken a task of mighty proportions. Eight hundred thousand homeless people, civilian victims of the war with newly created Israel, lived in camps on both sides of the Jordan River, in Lebanon and in Syria.

Leila's strength and dedication could be traced back to her grandmother, whose eldest child was twenty-five years old when her husband died in 1920. Leila was a young girl, but observant enough to see the wear and tear that nine boys had inflicted on one tiny, energetic woman. Leila was impressed with her grandmother's unceasing concern for the well-being and education of her children. Three of her sons were among the first college-educated Palestinians. When Leila would ask her grandmother how she found the strength to carry on, the answer was always the same: "Where there's a will, there's a way. We must survive."

Leila's father, Muhammad Dajani, the fourth child, was fair-skinned, tall, and strong. He strove hard, and bought extensive properties and a large wholesale grocery in Jerusalem, selling to both Jewish and Arab shops before the 1948 takeover, becoming successful and wealthy.

Her mother, Amneh, also tall and strong, was olive-skinned and as lovely inside as she was outside. She was one of eleven children of the Alami family, who had moved from Palestine to Aleppo, Syria. When Leila's father was visiting the Alamis on business in 1920, he met Amneh.

Early marriages were the rule then, and with the blessings of both families, they married. Muhammad took Amneh to live in the family home in Jerusalem. His father died later that year. Jerusalem was then under the British Mandate, and people had become educated to Western ways. English was taught in the schools. There were refrigerators and telephones. Leila's family took a European vacation each year.

Leila herself was born in Jerusalem in 1935, the fourth of eight children. One morning in 1947, when Leila was twelve years old, her uncle Ahmad came to their house and told them to go to the airport to be taken to Egypt immediately. Leila's family was one of the few who could afford to fly in those days. Her father took money from the cash register, for there was no time to go to the bank. When Amneh asked how long they would be gone, Ahmad said they would be back in a week and would need only a small bag each. Her mother, who always sensibly kept her family's gold on her person in the form of jewelry, packed the silverware, and buried her precious jewels in the rice container. There was no need to take them with her for such a short trip. Leila would never forget that Tuesday morning. They were gone for four years.

Other wealthy families, recognizing trouble, did the same, following the time-honored custom of the desert by going elsewhere until the crisis was over. Nearly a million of her less fortunate countrymen were forcibly expelled during the rise of Zionist terrorism and the breakdown of law and order during the last few months of the British Mandate.[1]

British authority deteriorated rapidly with the announcement of its departure from Palestine, and fighting spread throughout the region as normal administrative processes stopped functioning. While the Zionists had in place the Haganah, their underground army, and were defiantly arming themselves, Arab peasants remained vulnerable because of strict measures enforced by the British against carrying arms. The Arab Legion might have maintained order but was directed by the

War Office to stay out until the British left completely. When this occurred, on May 15, 1948, and the Legion finally managed to occupy what it could of the Arab zone, many rushed to seek refuge behind it. A few weeks later, its ammunition nearly depleted, the Legion evacuated Ramle and Lydda, a region that held at least 200,000 Arabs, including innumerable numbers of refugees from Jaffa and its environs.[2] Soon thereafter, the mayor of Ramle was advised secretly by a prominent Jew of his acquaintance to leave with his people since 'on the Israeli side things had got out of hand and the terrorists were in power,'[3] "... and no one could be responsible for what might occur," as Sir Geoffrey Furlonge references in the book *Palestine Is My Country: The Story of Musa Alami*. This caused another panic, and the Legion's troops were "overwhelmed by an avalanche of refugees arriving on foot, having been stripped of all they possessed, even down to the women's wedding rings, before they were allowed to leave."[4] Since military transport could not be spared, the refugees were forced to walk to the nearest place of refuge, Ramallah, which was miles away. "It was the height of summer and burning hot, and no one will ever know how many children died on the way."[5] The exodus continued all summer. Most went down to the Jordan Valley, which had water and a climate similar to the coastal plain. Almost a million people, most of them "respectable and decent peasants," according to Furlonge, "were now homeless and penniless wanderers, dependent on what the international organisations and other Arab Governments could do, eked out by day-to-day charity from neighbours who usually had little themselves to give."[6]

Meanwhile, Leila's family, thinking the problem would soon be resolved, rented a two-room apartment in Cairo. Half the family lived in one room, half in the other. When about six months had passed, and there was still no solution in sight, half the family took both rooms, and the rest moved to other quarters. Then Leila's twenty-year-old brother became seriously ill. From then on they thought only of going home; he wanted so much to die in his own land. But he died of heart failure in Cairo six months later. Another brother then got sick as a result of the rheumatic fever he had contracted soon after their flight to Egypt, and he asked his mother to go back, telling her he did not want his grave in Egypt. Leila's mother insisted on returning to Palestine. She couldn't face the loss of more children in a strange land, and begged her husband to allow them to die in their own country. Her brother died two months after their return, after choosing the place where he wished to be buried. When the family returned to East Jerusalem in 1951, their businesses, their lands, even their bank—all of which were now located in the occupied territory of West Jerusalem—had been confiscated by the Israelis. Everything was gone.

All her uncles, a sister, brother, and their families came to Jerusalem shortly thereafter. With bank loans from Jordan, her father started a wheat and grain business in Jordan, and with three of his brothers formed the Dajani Company, which thrived. He then rented a hotel from a convent, began the first cinema for children in Jerusalem in one of the hotel rooms, and rented the remaining rooms to tourists. He and his wife helped families who had lost their breadwinners during the war, Amneh providing housing and groceries for many of their neighbors, Muhammad helping societies and providing scholarships to poor students.

At first they lived in an old house inside the walled city of Jerusalem owned by Leila's grandfather—eight people in one big room for two years. Then they rented an apartment in Shu'fat, a village on the way to Ramallah. Leila graduated from the Schmidt School, then spent two years at home helping her mother, who by then was suffering from heart disease. Throughout this period, Leila was a daily witness to the compassion and generosity of her parents. Both were committed to their people, to a way of life they had lost, and to the return of their country. Leila had become a beautiful young woman, with the character of her father and the heart of her mother.

One uncle, a surgeon, was president of a hospital in Jerusalem. There for an appendectomy, Leila heard the nurses talking about Dr. Yahya Wahbeh, who worked at the hospital and who was one of the few pediatricians in Palestine. They spoke repeatedly of his kindness, skill, and graciousness. Leila then spent a few weeks at her uncle's house, next door to the hospital, recovering from the operation. Yahya heard about her through the same nurses and his grandmother, and asked her uncle if he could call on her. He began coming to breakfast and dinner. They visited for several weeks. She learned he was a man of principle, who respected and helped people regardless of nation or religion. After a while, he asked her father for her hand. Several men had asked to marry her, and she had refused. When Yahya asked, she accepted, telling her family she respected him because he was the kind of man who would always give more than he took. He fit her philosophy very well. He had a bank of goodness, which was to her far more important than money.

They married in 1957, when Leila was twenty-two. Theirs was the first hotel wedding in the city. Yahya continued his work at the government health department, the hospital, and his private office.

All went calmly until the 1967 War and her husband's deportation to Jordan. At about one o'clock in the morning of October 28, 1968, Leila was awakened by the sound of roaring engines. She peered through the curtain and saw several army jeeps with Israeli soldiers jumping from them, some of whom were gathering in the front garden while others spread around the house. She awakened Yahya, who dressed quickly and ran to the balcony. The doorbell began ringing insistently. Yahya and Leila opened the door, and a soldier pushed his way in, followed by several more behind him. The first soldier told Yahya he was wanted for a short time at army headquarters. When Yahya asked why, he was told only to hurry, and that he would know everything soon enough.

Had he not been big of heart, there would have been no trouble. But Dr. Wahbeh, instead of ignoring the plight of the refugees, had begged them to stay in their homes. When, out of fear for their lives, they refused, he cared for them—obtained food, blankets, and medical supplies and helped them live. The children knew their father would be taken sooner or later, because the Israeli authorities had been taking other doctors to jail or deporting them. Thousands of fathers and mothers were already in prison.

It was exceptionally cold that night. Yahya put on a pullover and an overcoat, then went down the stairs, surrounded by the soldiers. Leila stood at the balcony and saw him get into one of the five jeeps, watching until they all pulled away.

Stupefied, she sat on the sofa gazing vacantly at the wall, imagining what could happen to Yahya and wondering if she would ever see him again. As the room lightened, she realized that dawn had approached. She awakened ten-year-old Zaki, her eldest son, and told him the Israelis had taken his father. They cried together. Then, gathering her courage for his sake, she told him, "Zaki, be resolute. You are now the father of the family. Go to the mayor and tell him what has happened."

Just then the phone rang. It was Abu Saleh, the mayor of Al-Bireh, who said he had just had a news bulletin and that Dr. Wahbeh had been deported to Jordan. She told him what had occurred and that her son had just been about to go and tell him. "All of us will be driven out of our homeland!" she cried.

It was a perilous time. A war was going on. Leila had to manage all aspects of the family's life. Her youngest child was three years old.

She was enraged by the living conditions of the people who had been rounded up into camps: Babies were dying. There were no bathing facilities. Water for cooking was being carried for blocks, and cooking facilities were primitive. Moreover, there was little rice and bread to eat. She became convinced that it was up to the wealthy to motivate the poor, who were too immersed in staying alive to fight for much more. Her friends among the rich were more than willing to help with donations. Leila alone was willing to go to the camps and follow through, to deal with the red tape involved in making sure that donations reached their right destinations. She alone was willing to expend the time and energy necessary to be sure that the money or clothing or medical assistance was given to the people most in need of it.

Meanwhile, the people of Jerusalem went to the military authorities to ask for Yahya's return, to no avail. They demonstrated in the mosque. Men, women, and children marched through the streets, calling for him to be brought back to Al-Bireh.

The mayors of Al-Bireh and Ramallah persuaded Leila to continue her work when she despaired. They gave her the idea of getting people to help her. They taught her to help the people in the camps by taking them with her to the factories and having them ask for help and materials for their projects. The same people who went with her to ask did the work. She learned that when they created it, obtained it, and did the work themselves, they cared for it more. Abu Saleh, the mayor of Al-Bireh, was her inspiration. He helped her to keep her faith that she would be reunited with her husband. Shortly thereafter, the mayor himself was deported, along with several others.

Even then she was a reformer. When circumstances were against her, when she might be taken away at any time, her crusade for the poor continued. In Al-Bireh, there was a charitable organization caring for orphan children through kindergarten. The children appeared to be weak and undernourished. It was suggested that Leila become a member to see what was happening to the children. She found they were being fed very little. Only when members of the government came to visit did the staff cook. The donations were going not to the charity's aim, but into the pockets of some of the members. She took them to court. The charity was disbanded, and a new society was established for elderly women with no one to care for them. The children were sent to relatives.

By joining charities and sewing centers, Leila heard stories. When fathers died, mothers sent their children to orphanages and went to work. Leila went to their houses to see if they really needed help. It was through the children that she met the mothers. Since only about 20 percent of Palestinian widows remarried, most women had to support their children for most, if not all, of their lives. Leila's primary concern was to obtain jobs for the widows. Once a woman was working, Leila was free to go to the next needy family.

Two years after her husband's deportation, Leila received a letter from a friend who told her Yahya had been in a car accident and was in the hospital with damaged discs in his neck. The authorities gave her a pass to go to him because he needed care. She took the children. Allowed to stay only two weeks, she went back to Jerusalem. In order to return to Jordan she was required to provide proper identity papers for herself and their children, but the Israeli government refused to issue them. At last, Leila was told that if she obtained the signatures of forty doctors guaranteeing that Dr. Wahbeh would not leave, he could return. She did so, and Yahya returned to his Public Health Department position.

When at last they settled in Amman she continued her crusade, driving herself relentlessly. She created a society for orphans. She uncovered and publicized the horrors of camp living wherever she found them. Through donations from merchants and friends, her energy, and her conviction that her people must survive, the lives of many in the camps slowly began to change.

She selected sites for community centers, deciding with the affected people on the building design, the landscaping, and the ministries to solicit for donations of land. Her people must have trees and flowers. She demanded cleanliness. Her people must live decently and with dignity.

Leila went further and decided to tackle problems affecting schoolchildren of all ages. With a twofold purpose in mind, she took them to the camps to aid in her construction projects and to the orphanages. In this way, children with more taught those with less, and they themselves learned to treat others with kindness and to establish camaraderie among them. As children do, they told their parents, and they in turn contacted Leila to ask if she wanted help. Leila asked them to accompany her, to see for themselves as their children had. The parents went with her, and from that seed thousands of families began to feel a kinship with their people. That sense of community continues today. Some families sent orphans to university or kept them on holidays. Others helped to support them until they were able to work. As Leila often said, "One small stone in the water creates thousands of ripples."

She built houses for widows who were ill, and whose families were on the West Bank and couldn't help them. After heavy rains, when houses slid away, she took parents and friends to see the devastation. All the materials were donated, and the people in the camps rebuilt their houses.

Leila found parents for orphans, wrote letters to relatives for the illiterate, and distributed food and clothing. Over the next fourteen years, she visited four camps regularly and traveled fifty to a hundred kilometers a day, taking foreigners and anyone who would go with her to gain sympathy and publicity for camp conditions. She became well-known to all the embassies and schools. Her phone never stopped ringing with pleas for help.

Then, suddenly, she decided to change her methods of work. She no longer had the patience to work within societies. It took too long between the pleas for help and the solution to the problem. There were too many people whose permission was required, too many meetings where too little was accomplished, and too much talk of fashion, makeup, or hairstyles.

"I am not interested in fashion," she would say. "My dresses will take me from morning to night. I put them on. I comb my hair. What else do I need?

"Charities start raising money. Sometimes it doesn't go to the people who are in need. It goes for dinners and gifts to those who are not in need. I have no time for those who have nothing on their minds but how they appear from their heads to their shoes.

"If I work as a member of a charity, I must carry the name of the charity. Instead I see who is really in need. The mother looks poor. There is no money to buy medicine. If she is really poor, I can help her by taking rich people to her. If you want to help people, see their house, ask their neighbor, see how you can help them. Don't donate money to everyone who comes to you. You visit them. Donations become habit-forming. People need to stand on their own two feet and find work. Don't teach them to beg."

Too often she acted on these principles without concern or fear of the consequences. She was to learn that donations are not always given from the heart. Finally convinced by her family not to accept money, she accepted only goods and services directly through donors who accompanied her to the sites. She showed each donor exactly how to spend his or her money and exactly where it should be going.

Undaunted by delays, red tape, and discomfort, Leila continued to respond to the unending requests for help. In one year alone, her work bore the fruit of 200,000 dinars in goods and services. Not a penny changed hands.

"A well-fed family is a happy family," Leila would say. "That is my principle." With the early breakfast meal finished, the dinner on the stove, and the kitchen spotless, she was on her way. All her movements were quick and vigorous. Her mind raced ahead of each activity, planning, preparing, solving. After she fed her family each afternoon, she finally relaxed in the lovely cocoon of tranquility she had created.

When asked by those awed by her incredible energy and determination how she could continue when the problem was overwhelming, her answer was always the same.

"You must never say 'impossible.' You must never say 'I am tired' or 'disgusted' or 'frustrated.' You must say you *did* something. When you give one day from your life to make many families happy, you are adding to your bank. You are the bridge of happiness. These good things are the assets in my bank. They are better than money. I am rich."

And then she'd laugh—a melodic, joyful laugh.

CHAPTER FOUR

A Bank of Goodness

War preceded or followed Yahya wherever he happened to be. He was born four years after World War I in Jerusalem, one of five children. His parents, Zakaria Wahbeh and Thuraya Abdo, were close relatives. They married in 1920 in Bab Hutta Square in the Old City of Jerusalem.

By the end of World War II, Yahya had met all the necessary qualifications for pre-med and was ready for medical school. Tuition in Egypt was free for Palestinian students at the time, and donations given by the Red Crescent Society helped with other school expenses. To cover his personal costs, he worked as a statistician while attending school.

He'd completed his education at Alexandria University in Egypt and one year of his internship in 1951, when the country was threatened with a coup d'état. A middle ranking officer, Gamal Abdel Nasser, was inciting the young officers to overthrow the monarchy. His fury at his troops being given faulty weapons and boomeranging explosives in the 1948 War with Israel had not abated. The supply scandal had involved members of the royal family. King Farouk, who controlled Egypt and the Sudan, felt his position was strong because he'd be protected by the British Army. Yahya decided to go home before the situation worsened. He was wise to do so. The 1952 revolt led by Nasser ended the monarchy. Farouk fled the country for Italy, taking with him ninety suitcases filled with treasure.

Yahya's trip home was arduous. The only flights were on small seven-passenger planes. He took a ship from Alexandria, first to Cypress then to Beirut, Lebanon. From there he took a bus to Damascus, Syria, then to Amman, Jordan, and finally a taxi to Jerusalem. A trip that would take two hours by plane today, took him twelve hours.

Finally, the familiar arch over the entrance to his family home appeared. Its support distinguished it from all the neighboring entrances and prevented it from being torn down. Long ago it had been designated Waqf property, meaning property that cannot be sold or privately owned and thereby always available to anyone in the family in need. He wasn't allowed to enter. In his absence, his home had been confiscated by the Israelis. Yahya's heart sank. That day, the first of many disappointments, was one of the hardest to bear. He had to stop thinking of returning to the warmth and welcome of the home that had been in his family for 300 years.

His family had joined his uncle's family in Beir Zeit, a village close to Ramallah, when the 1948 War began. Eight people were living in that house. Yahya decided to go to Bethlehem. He was assigned by the Health Department to a local hospital as a house officer, first practicing in all sections of the hospital, and then as a resident practicing in only one section. While he worked, he studied for his exams in Egypt, obtained his degree, and became a pediatrician. It was there that he met and worked with Leila's uncle, Dr. Dajani.

In 1955 he met Leila. His grandmother had been her family's neighbor in Jerusalem, and she recommended that Yahya marry Leila, whom she described as being faithful and active. He'd also heard about Leila from the nurses in the hospital and from her uncle, who told Yahya he would find Leila a great help in his work. It was arranged that they should meet.

She was to Yahya many things in one. He found her to be benevolent and sympathetic with the needy, and she was courageous, hard working, impulsive, good-tempered, and kind. Besides all this, she could ride a bicycle. He found that charming.

They were married on July 5, 1957, in her father's hotel. Yahya had waited to marry until he finished his medical education, was employed, and properly prepared for the duties of life, proving once again his steadiness and reliability. After their marriage, he urged Leila to help their people, believing that no matter what she did, it would have a good result. When she put her mind to something, things went smoothly and quickly. Yahya urged her to think things over for a day or two, but Leila acted very swiftly, especially if the matter was serious. She decided that if what she'd done was right, she was willing to accept the consequences.

Yahya continued working in Bethlehem at the Department of Health and in his private practice. In 1959 he transferred to Ramallah Hospital, again spending his afternoons with private patients. He was earning good money, and they were doing well. They had four children: Zaki in 1958, Maysoon in 1959, Monia in 1962, and Amjad in 1965.

Then came disaster in the form of the 1967 War between the Arabs and the Zionists of Israel, later termed the Six-Day War. Israelis occupied the West Bank and the city of Jerusalem. It was a very hard time. Schools closed for months. Initially, curfew was imposed day and night, then only at night to avoid attacks by the invading army. There was no travel allowed between villages or outside the country. People were arrested without charge and tortured. Since imports were halted, there were food and medicine shortages. It happened that Yahya was head of the Red Crescent Society in Ramallah in collaboration with the Red Cross. The Ministry of Health had decreed in 1965 that doctors could not have a private practice and also work in government. Yahya closed his practice and concentrated on public service, believing it would be better for the country. After the Six-Day War, 20,000 displaced people from the Latroun District, the southern district of Ramallah, came to the city of Ramallah. Their villages had been razed by Israeli bulldozers and were then proclaimed a "no man's land" and renamed Canada Park. Some of the villagers died under their collapsing houses. Leila found clothing and housing for all the displaced persons. To keep them in the Ramallah District, the Red Crescent Society also provided support.

One day a demonstration was held against displacing those villagers. Some female students participated. Yahya was out on an errand. As he neared the crowd, he slowed his car. Two girls jumped into the back seat asking him to take them away from the Israeli soldiers who were dispersing the demonstration. Then a man jumped into the front passenger seat, also asking to taken away from the crowd. Yahya noticed his strange accent. The next day a man came to their home, claiming to belong to the resistance. He asked for food, but left hurriedly upon Yahya's return. A day later, Leila spotted the same man in an Israeli army truck with the Israeli soldiers. Two days later, at midnight, their house in Al-Bireh City near Ramallah was surrounded by the Israeli Army. Yahya was taken for detention to army headquarters until dawn, then by army jeep to the Allenby Bridge in Jericho, a journey of an hour and a half. Deportation was commonly used by the Israelis to remove unwanted people from the country. Yahya planned to contact the Red Cross in Amman. Since he was head of the Red Crescent Society, which cooperated with the Red Cross, he wasn't afraid. He was resigned to being unable to return to his country.

Meanwhile, Leila called the mayor of Al-Bireh with the news of Yahya's arrest. He immediately notified the media. At 7 a.m., the Israeli Commissioner announced on the radio the following: "In accordance with the law of military regulations, Dr. Y. Wahbeh was against the State of Israel and was deported from the West Bank of Israel to the East Bank, the country of Jordan."

Yahya's crime was that he'd established a factory for the displaced people to make rugs, so they could earn enough money to live. This was against policy, of course. The Israelis did not want any Arabs to have jobs. They wanted them to be forced off their land and out of their country. When the bulletin was released over the radio that Dr. Wahbeh had been detained and deported, Leila received it immediately. A cousin on the East Bank also heard the news and brought Yahya some clothing.

Forcibly separated from his family, he filled his days working with the Red Cross in Amman and in pediatrics at the hospital in Zarka, and his nights alone in a special room at the hospital. Most of his meals were taken at the hospital or at the homes of other doctors who'd befriended him. From time to time he visited family in Amman, his brother, sister, uncle, and brother-in-law. There was no way to communicate with his family or to send them money except by friends who traveled between Amman and occupied Palestine.

When he wasn't working, Yahya used the time to study the different species of scorpions and traveled throughout Jordan searching for them. He'd begun working on scorpion research in the early 1950s. Many children died from scorpion stings, and there was no specific treatment against the scorpions of the region. He wrote to the manufacturers of the serum at Pasteur Institute in Tunisia and began a campaign to identify the scorpion species in Jordan. His research included extracting the venom and defining its toxicity. Students accompanied him on his search for scorpions, one or two classes at a time going with him to the field. His research then led to injecting the venom into lab rats and mice to learn the toxicity. He delivered the samples he'd collected to the Lister Institute in England and Pasteur Institute in Paris. His research resulted in identifying the Jordanian species and their venom toxicity and the correct treatment of sting victims. (He received the Jordan Medical Association Award in 1973.) In his absence, Leila cared for and taught the children with help of family and friends and continued her humanitarian aid to the refugees of Al-Bireh.

Finally, in 1971 she and the children received a permit to visit Yahya from time to time during school breaks. At last in 1973 they joined him permanently. Yahya noticed that Leila had changed during their separation. She was more patient, more aware of the consequences of her behavior. He, too, had changed, becoming more cautious. Both were even more appreciative of the other and their families. They rented a three-bedroom, second-floor apartment in Webdeh, on one of Amman's seven mountains, and furnished it with items they'd brought by truck from Al-Bireh. The children were happy for the reunion with Yahya, and that at last they could spend time with him. Many of the doctors and others who'd been deported were already friends, so the adjustment was easier than it might have been otherwise. The children attended private schools, which then were moderately priced, until college.

In 1983, when only Maysoon remained at home, they moved to the physicians' condominiums where I met them. The plane crash in 1977 that killed Queen Alia, the Minister of Health, an army doctor, and the pilot, had changed Yahya's position. His services were needed at the University of Jordan Hospital, so for two years he was both pediatrician and administrative director of the hospital. In 1979 he went back to pediatrics at Al-Ashrafia Hospital in Amman. After a year as administrative director, he retired and has since been under contract to the medical college of the University of Jordan, doing projects or research sponsored by different agencies. Today, at eighty-nine years, Yahya's work continues. He drives. His hearing is excellent. His conversations are as engaging as ever. His most recent discovery, an ointment for the treatment of bed sores and trigger finger ailment, will come to market this year.

He attributes his patience and good nature to his beloved grandmother, who took him with her wherever she went. Her benevolence taught him to care for others, not just physically but emotionally and financially as well. His uncle, a tour guide in Palestine, was also a mentor. From him he learned kindness to strangers and how to listen no matter how long or circuitous the story. How well these traits have served him during his life's travails. No wonder he has emerged sound of mind and spirit.

CHAPTER FIVE

We Would Give You Our Blood

JUST BEFORE OUR RETURN TO AMMAN IN OCTOBER 1983, Leila had embarked on a new and much needed project—the creation of sanitation centers to replace the eleven huge refuse dumps scattered throughout Baqa'a Camp. When I called to say we had arrived, Leila was eager that I begin accompanying her on her daily rounds. Since she accomplished more in eight hours than most people I knew did in a month, I was mentally and physically prepared for a rigorous and fascinating time. I couldn't wait to share my good news with her. It had taken a great deal of time and effort to find merchants willing to buy goods they wouldn't see for several months from a woman who was leaving the country for an undetermined length of time, but I had done it and had in hand 1,000 dollars' worth of orders for the widows to complete. I hadn't written my news, because I wanted to see Leila's expression when I told her I had succeeded in opening a market for her people to display their talents.

As we drove to Baqa'a the next morning to check that all the refuse had been removed from the site, and to meet with the building committee, I made my announcement. Instead of the enthusiastic response I had anticipated, she matter-of-factly said, "Very well." I'd expected glowing praise, and I got "very well"? That was it? Taken aback, I thought about it for a few minutes, and then smiled to myself. Of course. It was a foregone conclusion that I would follow through, and that I would succeed. When did Leila suffer underachievers?

I was brought back to the day's activities.

"I have asked for a large work crew to help with the grading and paving of the area where the sanitation center will be built. I have to know what time I can count on the people starting, because students will be brought from Amman to assist in completing the work."

"For you, Leila, they'll be there with bells on," I assured her. Leila also told me that she had the donation of a grader and operator, but that we had to find someone within the camp to donate the cement for the sewage channel.

When we pulled up to the site, the workers all greeted us cordially, and Leila introduced me to each of the men, one of whom was Mustafa. I was dazzled by his movie-star looks—flashing brown eyes; olive skin; wavy dark hair with streaks of gray; tall, lithe frame; and winsome smile. His English was quite good. When I asked his age, he told me he was twenty-five, younger than my own son. Later I would learn he had lived twice his age.

Leila motioned Mustafa and his cousin to follow us in their car, and we set out to find the donor Mustafa had suggested. It was no easy task in the patchwork of byways, but find him Leila did, by leaning out the car window at every crossroad and asking his name of the pedestrians who crowded the muddy roads. When we found his tiny house, we waited until Mustafa had parked his car and joined us for our visit. It took only a few minutes for Leila to convince the generous man to donate tons of cement for the next day's project. We returned to the car, only to find a flat tire. Mustafa and his cousin quickly replaced it with the spare and rolled her tire to their car. "Leila, wait!" I said anxiously, having heard stories of thievery in the camps. "Don't let them go away with your tire. We must stay with them."

She looked at me, puzzled by my concern. "My tire will be fixed. It will be waiting for me tomorrow. Do not worry." Calmly, secure in her knowledge that I would eventually learn about her people, she allayed my fears. A week or so later, it was time for a progress check. The heat was intense. There was no air conditioning in the car, and it was stifling. To take my mind off my nausea and the sweat running down my back, I asked Leila why she had decided to tackle the enormous garbage problem that beset Baqa'a. Her reply revealed that it wasn't the only problem.

"I was working on the sewage, building channels, you know. A man owned a truck and said he wanted to help. He began working with the men. I offered to pay him forty dinars, Pat. He said he didn't want money. I was astonished! His name was Abdullah. Mustafa, his nephew, lives in the same house. I insisted on visiting him. He was not at home, so I sat with his family and asked how he could donate help when his family was living in a two-by-three-meter space and was in such need. I asked his wife how she could live with an open garbage dump outside her house and those all around her. The wife said, 'Find us a solution. UNRWA doesn't help us. Please, Umm Zaki, help us. I have sick children. The sick reports say it is from the garbage.' I told the wife I would see. The family said, 'We will help. For sixteen years, nobody listens. Nobody will solve this problem.'"

Leila was silent a few moments, maneuvering through traffic. "I asked the family what they needed. The wife said, 'Nobody helps us.' She showed me many children. They had cysts on their faces, discharges in their eyes. Children fell from the top of the garbage heap and broke their bones. 'When bones break,' the wife told me, 'they are not properly set, and the children are crippled. UNRWA gives very little treatment. Some of the children are burned or poisoned while playing in the garbage.'"

Leila spotted a roadside vendor. We pulled up, bought soft drinks, and were quickly on our way. She resumed her story.

"What can I do, Pat? I took a performance contract to UNRWA, guaranteeing to pay for the work, and offered to help build a sanitation center. A building with a door and a roof, with covered trash containers, with lights to keep the rabbits away."

"Rabbits, Leila? You have rabbits here?" Then it dawned on me. "What do they look like?"

"You know," she answered, impatient. "Rabbits. Sharp teeth, long tails."

"No, Leila." I shook my head. "Rabbits have long ears. *Rats* have long tails."

"We killed hundreds of rats," she announced, "with the shovels." Revulsion washed over me.

"We wanted pine trees to provide some shade, with a play area around it for the children. I went to a contractor to ask how much it would cost. He said 8,000 dinars for sewage channels, the sanitation center, and the play area. It is too much money. The women said they would write letters to UNRWA asking for the building and saying they would help put it up. UNRWA gave permission. Many came to help start the work, and from them I made a committee of five men in the affected area. Mustafa was one of them. He came to me and said, 'I am an engineer. I work in a factory and would like to help you solve the garbage problem.' I was pleased for his help. He quickly went to government headquarters and followed the papers through to get permission. The next day, we sat together and studied the situation. Without taking any money, he made a plan of the building area and started the cost analysis. He was the first man who worked and the first volunteer. Pat, he even took a leave of absence from work without pay! Every day he was at my house at 8 a.m.

and visited the factories with me. We found other companies that handled the building materials we needed and spent one week visiting them. We took the scale model with us and showed pictures of children playing on the garbage. He told the owners what we needed. Most gave immediately, and their trucks of donated materials followed us to the project. We went every day for two weeks. If, on the way, we saw something we needed, we told the factories about it. They brought it. In two weeks, the people from the camp were working, and we were getting what we needed. Children, some only five to eight years old, helped carry the cement blocks. We built a channel to drain the sewage.

"I rested at Mustafa's house. Women came to tell me their problems. 'Umm Zaki, I have a child who needs medicine and the hospital.' I found a doctor to operate. The child is progressing.

"'Please, Umm Zaki, I have nothing. I have nine children. Can you find me work?' There is a place beside us. I saw the owner. She has a job now and earns three dinars daily. She says, 'Thank you very much.' Another tells me her husband suffers. She cannot buy anything because the medicine is too expensive. I send her to the factory of medicine to get him what he needs. I get her transportation to guarantee she would go. In this way, we solve not only the garbage problem, but hundreds and thousands of problems."

What she was saying was incredible, but I knew it was true. I had seen enough with my own eyes to know how much change she had brought about. Thousands of problems were solved by Leila, who was simply "paying her taxes."

As the floor and sides of the building went up, our trips to the site became more frequent. Each visit required a conference with the group, all of whom beamed with pride each time we approached. The children thrust their arms through the open car windows and began pulling on us, to be the first to point out the most recent change. Most of the discussion was in Arabic, so Leila translated the pertinent parts. "See how far we have come, Umm Zaki?" was the most frequent refrain.

A month later, the fateful date arrived. Leila told me that all that was left to do was to find roofing material. The lighting would be donated by a doctor.

On the way to the site, she spotted some rusting beams beside the highway. Turning at seventy kilometers an hour from the far right lane to the factory on the left side of the highway, she screeched to a halt, trotted into the building in her long, black, embroidered dress and plastic sandals, convinced the factory owner the beams were usable, and obtained his agreement to bring them to the camp for the center. Then we continued our journey.

As we neared the camp, I told Leila I had been thinking about Mustafa a great deal. "I can't believe he actually took off work to assist you in this project. Doesn't he need the money? Won't his employer fire him?"

"No, Pat. His employer is Palestinian. He wants to help his people, too, you see? These people are not lazy. They don't want things done for them. They want to help themselves. They simply don't have the money to start. If someone can guarantee the payment of the work, there is nothing they won't do to improve their circumstances. I am fortunate enough to know many people who are willing to donate materials. That's how I can guarantee payment and completion. The people themselves will complete it. Think of Mustafa, Pat. My son has a car. He visits his friends. They live in palaces. Could Mustafa invite anyone to his house with all that garbage outside the door? Can he go to the school of his choice? Of course not. Without a scholarship, he would never have become an engineer. Without brothers to support him through school, he could never have attended. Do you see the difference? We must make that difference go away. Opportunity must be available to anyone with the determination and intelligence to succeed."

We pulled up to the site. The area was spotless. The grader had prepared the ground for asphalt, the floor and sides of the center were finished, and the sewage channels had been dug and cemented. The volunteers' work had paid off handsomely. Mountains of refuse had been replaced by gravel glistening as brightly as if the women had polished each individual stone.

When Leila told the crowd that the lighting was forthcoming and that the roofing would arrive the next day, all agreed to gather the necessary work detail. Mustafa led everyone in thanking Leila, and asked us into his uncle's house. Leila listened to the problems of the women who came and went, including that of a young widow. Her husband had been killed in an accident after only four months of marriage. She had her teaching certificate, but no money and no place to live, as they had been living temporarily with his already overburdened family. Leila took her name and said she would do her best to solve the problem.

It was time to move on. Mustafa said his leave from work would be finished upon completion of the roof, and that if Leila needed him for anything else, he was always ready to help.

We left his house. From a large crowd gathered around the car, two women came forward unfurling a large piece of black velvet like a banner so that Leila could read the words that had been painstakingly stitched onto the fabric in tiny gold sequins.

"It is for you, Umm Zaki. Mustafa said we should wait until the frame is finished, but after your news today, we couldn't wait. It will be completed by your next visit."

Leila read the message aloud to me: "Thanks to God for sending you to us, Umm Zaki. We would give you our blood."

They stood quietly, gazing at Leila with such fondness and such pride in themselves that a lump came to my throat. After the backbreaking labor these women had performed during construction, they had cheerfully toiled for countless more hours to create a message that no famous artist's work could equal. Leila smiled and took the hands of the oldest woman in the crowd and thanked all of them for their kindness and help.

When we had inched our way past pedestrians to the highway, I asked Leila where she would hang her treasure.

"Will it help my people by hanging it in my living room? Will it help my people for my visitors to read it? Will it impress my family? No."

"But Leila! It's an expression of their feelings for you! Don't you think they mean for you to hang it where you can think of them every time you look at it?"

"No, Pat," she answered in a tone that indicated extreme patience with my mental capacities. "I will carefully pluck out my name from the message. Then I will take it to the office of a very rich man and tell him that these words are from his people for his generous donations. Other men will visit his offices. They will read the words and will wish they had such a message. The rich man will be very proud. When I ask him for donations in the future, he will be even more generous. And those who read his message will ask to contribute."

She was silent then, giving me time to absorb the lesson. After a while, I reached over and squeezed her hand, contrite. Once again she had forced me to see things in a new way. It was at that moment that I knew how much I loved her.

When we arrived in Amman, we stopped at an orphanage Leila had created. She talked with the director, while I sipped Turkish coffee. When we left, the young widow we had met at Mustafa's house that morning had a job and room and board, starting immediately. Once again, thanks to Leila's zeal, the helpless had become the helpful.

1998 – Mustafa married and left the camp. He was hired by a construction company as an architect. His wife teaches at a private school. They have three children.

CHAPTER SIX

Will You Celebrate?

The phone rang. It was Leila. She came right to the point.

"Hello, Pat. I'll pick you up in the morning. Please. Tell Lee it will be a very busy day and that you won't be back soon. We have many errands, and we are going to a graduation of Palestinian boys in the late afternoon, so wear hose and a dress with sleeves. Plan to have lunch with me."

She arrived very early, with Mustafa in tow. As it was already hot, I asked them to sit down and gave them a cold drink. After relaxing for a moment, Leila asked me to show Mustafa some drawings I had bought a few days before.

"Mustafa must know what people like to buy."

"Mustafa," I said delighted. "I know you are an engineer. You're an artist as well?"

"Ah, I am an engineer and very good in art also."

I brought out prints by David Roberts, a nineteenth-century artist who had lived in the Middle East and whose paintings of Arab life have become classics.

"This is what people like to see, Mustafa," I said, shuffling the prints before him. "Pictures of your people at work, at play, and at rest. Let the world know how you spend your time, whether it's buying produce, weaving, making coffee, dancing. It doesn't matter, as long as the pictures are true to your traditions. Don't exaggerate or try to make them look Western."

"Pat, we must find a way to give him a show. What do you think?" Leila's expression suggested a *fait accompli*.

"It isn't easy. Local shops and galleries may not agree with our taste in art. We must get the opinion of a well-known local gallery before Mustafa expends a great effort. If his work is of a style that appeals to this market as well as to foreigners, the gallery will tell us if they wish to represent him. If Amman is like the States, the gallery will take a large commission and give Mustafa what is left. He must be prepared to be persistent." Mustafa's expression told me I had dampened his enthusiasm.

Leila was pensive for a moment. Then she smiled a smile I was beginning to know only too well, and stood up.

"Are you ready?" Mustafa and I glanced at each other. It was just past the crack of dawn. It was sweltering. Why wouldn't we be ready?

Mustafa followed us in his car. Our first stop was the American School. We went to the library, where Vivian, slide projector in hand, rushed by, saying, "I must go to my first graders. The clothes are in the teachers' lounge."

We discovered several boxes and large trash bags of clothing, shoes, and games. Leila deftly separated them into two stacks, one for the people who had helped with the sanitation center, and one for a couple whose son, Bassam, was graduating from high school that afternoon. Mustafa put the clothes for the camp into his car and followed us to a center for the speech and hearing impaired where he could look at paintings I had admired on an earlier visit and get an idea of what Westerners find interesting about Middle Eastern culture. That done, Leila announced we had more stops to make. I had long since given up asking beforehand the whys and wherefores of our expeditions; the purpose changed depending on prevailing crises.

Mustafa then left us to fetch a wheelchair from another friend of Leila's who donated it so that a crippled lady could attend her mother's funeral on the West Bank. The chair would be of use because the lines were long and conditions uncomfortable at the Israeli border crossing of the Jordan River. Mustafa would meet us later.

We stopped to pick up Leila's cousin, Fatima, a short, dark, lively, middle-aged woman. She spoke no English, so Leila told me about her. She had returned to Amman from Egypt when her sister died. The sister, mother of three boys, had also cared for her blind relatives. After her death, Fatima asked her husband to move back to Amman so she could care for the family. When he refused to leave his job in Egypt, she asked him to divorce her, and returned to raise the boys and maintain the rest of the household.

I found Fatima lying on a little cot in a bedroom, the fan blowing on her full force. The day was so hot that the walk down the several flights of outside steps to her apartment gate had drenched my blouse and straightened my hair. My chances of looking cool and poised at the graduation were quickly diminishing. Fatima and I hurried up the many steps back to the street, because Leila, as usual, was double-parked and honking. We'd barely got on our way when she suddenly stopped the car again, in a no-parking zone, gestured helplessness to the policemen, and sent me into a shop, telling me to pick up sixty dinars from the proprietor. Having by now become used to acting on the double when around Leila, I was back in the car in seconds, gasping for breath.

"Why did I do that?" I queried, hotter than ever.

"The owner of the Windy Shop, Miss Nazha Khairy, helps. She sells the pillow covers without taking a penny. She believes in helping the people who work to give them initiative. I have no time now to sell the products of the women. I take their work to this shop, and Miss Khairy sells them, just like Vivian."

Even the merchants were enlisted in Leila's projects. This one sold the finished pieces to foreign women who, frustrated, stopped trying to duplicate the cross-stitching they so admired. It gave Leila another opportunity to show the refugee artists that their work was appreciated and valuable.

Finally, we arrived at the Sukayna School for Girls to meet with the director, where Mustafa was waiting for us. We went directly to the library, passing hundreds of uniformed girls in the halls and on the steps. I asked Leila how many students there were.

"About a thousand Muslim girls from ages sixteen to eighteen transfer to this government secondary school after attending an UNRWA preparatory school from twelve to sixteen. All are bussed or walk from all the camps in Amman. Only 5 percent of the students are Christian, because Christian schools are available. None of these students can afford private school." She walked swiftly down the corridor.

"Why are we here?" *By this time I know better than to ask that,* I thought, as Mustafa and I trotted to catch up to Leila.

"First we are meeting Khitam Kaddomi, the librarian. She is taking me to the people who will donate the Arabic books for Souf and Baqa'a."

I was happy to find that the library was much like ours in American schools, with study tables, good lighting, and an excellent reference system. Shelf after shelf contained books on every subject; tantalizing displays of teenage fiction awaited eager eyes. I asked Mrs. Kaddomi if the library contained biographies. She assured me that it did, and that the books were about famous people throughout the world. The students received a broad education and would speak at least two languages by graduation. I asked why she was helping with the book donations.

"This is a well-equipped school. We have specialists in all areas of life, from engineers to doctors to librarians; all of us who live outside the camps must help those inside."

Leila pulled out her ever-present pictures to show the progress at the camp library. After viewing them and talking for a few moments, Mrs. Kaddomi led us to a large hall containing the home economics exhibit.

What a variety of crafts the girls learned during their two years at the school! Besides baked goods for sale, there were exhibits that included strikingly arranged wall displays of dresses, suits, skirts, and blouses. The fabrics and the sewing were of excellent quality, and even hard-to-work materials, such as taffetas, linens, and satins, were used for the party dresses. There were also items made of batik and macramé, as well as clay sculptures and many kinds of jewelry. Since ready-made items are very costly, the girls were being taught to beautify their homes through their own handiwork. Most would marry after high school and would probably not go on to college, because when six or seven members of a family have to work to support one child through college, it is most often a boy who is chosen, as he is expected later to support all of them.

After our tour, we were taken to the director, who was sitting with several other women in her office. I thought they were teachers on a break, but it turned out most were members of the mothers' council, who met with the director once a week to make suggestions and proposals. After introductions and my compliments to the director on the modern library and the unusually well-made displays by the home economics students, she introduced me to the women. Leila showed them her photos and held a spirited conversation in Arabic with the director. Mustafa sat next to me, very quiet, smoking, his eyes downcast. Leila stood up, ready to leave. Mustafa was going to Baqa'a and would meet us later.

"Did you see how nice everyone was?" Leila asked me as we walked out of the building to the car.

"Yes, but everyone is always nice."

"Ah, but no one said I could not keep Mustafa with me. He would never be allowed to enter a girls' school unless he was with me."

"Is it because of your dress? Because everyone recognizes you and realizes you're likely to have from one to twenty people with you?"

"My dress goes everywhere, and my friends with it. That is true." She laughed, then was silent. It gave her announcement more impact. "The school will have his art show."

"I don't believe it! You mean the visit to the director's office was to get the school to agree to a show by Mustafa?" I stopped near the car. Why was I surprised?

"Yes. It took us a month to build, to plant trees, and to get lights installed at our sanitation center at Baqa'a. The contractor told us 8,000 dinars, remember? We built it for nothing, because everything was donated. There are ten more dumps to clean up. Mustafa suggested he could help by having an art show, the proceeds of which would go to creating another center. That's why we went to the director's office. They will put on the show." She looked at me primly, and folded her arms in that way she had when all had gone according to her plan, kind of hugging herself.

"Leila, you are unbelievable! It isn't noon yet! What does the rest of the day hold in store?"

"Many things." I squeezed her arm. She granted me a small smile as she started the car. It faded quickly.

"The teachers you met this morning are coming to the graduation."

"How nice. Do the brothers of some of the girls go to the school?"

"No. It is because many of these boys are orphans. If we don't go, there will be no one in the audience for them. When I invited them to the celebration of the students from Palestine School, they said they were very busy. I told them many have no mother and father. Who will celebrate? These children have nobody. I must go. This is my tax. We must all go. I told them that when my daughter graduated last year, she had two parents. I left her father at her graduation and went to the Palestinian boys' graduation by myself. I told them they must be proud of themselves and proud of their people who will one day be back in their homes. They got tears in their eyes and agreed they would pay a little of their taxes by attending the celebration."

"Leila, you are shameless!"

"What is shameless?"

"It means you will do or say anything to get your people motivated into action, no matter how dramatic."

"That is my principle. Why should they sit at home and do nothing when they can help their people? No! They must help!" She pounded her fist on the steering wheel for emphasis.

We decided not to go to Leila's for lunch. The family would eat the food she had prepared before leaving for the day. Instead, we picked up *shawarma* sandwiches—lamb, onions, and spices wrapped in pita bread— from a street vendor and ate them on the way to Baqa'a to distribute the clothing from the American School. Mustafa greeted us. He had emptied all the bags into piles in his house so the women could come to one place to choose what they needed. After we were welcomed enthusiastically, Leila sent a little boy to a shop for soft drinks. Within moments, fifty women were gathered in the room. In a few more moments, the clothing was gone, and only the family and a few women remained. I motioned Mustafa to sit beside me, so he could answer some questions.

"Mustafa, you are an engineer. Couldn't you do anything about the garbage?"

"You were not here when the garbage was piled high outside the doors of these houses. You have seen the other dumps, so you know what we have experienced. You ask why the garbage stays here, why it is hauled here in wheelbarrows, why the loader comes to us only once a week, why we can do nothing." His tone took on a harsh edge. "This garbage remains because UNRWA needs donations. If there is nothing to show, there will be no donations. No donations, no money to keep the officials living well.

"You have asked me many questions since we met. Let me answer some of them before I tell you of my life. You want to know about health. I'll tell you about health. You know that in our country every woman wants sons. A neighbor has ten girls. At last she has a boy. Everyone is very happy. There is dancing in the street. The family has no money for doctors, so they must use a midwife from UNRWA. When the midwife brings the baby, she improperly ties the umbilical cord for the baby's stomach. The child dies in five hours."

I told Mustafa I had just visited UNRWA's offices and had obtained their literature. The brochures described the health and education programs at each of the camps and how they spent the money received from the member countries. America was listed as the largest contributor, giving 67 million dollars in 1983.

"Go home and tell them how their money is being spent," he said in quiet fury. "Tell someone what is really happening here."

"Mustafa, I went to UNRWA with the goal of checking all the printed materials against what I see with my own eyes. In that regard I am Leila's disciple. It has become my principle also to see for myself. With Leila's help and yours, I am seeing. We attend a large, progressive church in the States. If I can tell the congregation the truth, perhaps they will choose us as a social concerns project. If not, we will find other ways to get the donations directly to the people. My people and yours must be informed."

Leila reminded me we would have to leave for the graduation soon. I patted Mustafa's arm sympathetically and told him we would visit again within the week. He held out a ragged diary. "For years I have faithfully written my story. What I tell you will be true."

We stopped at Leila's on the way to the auditorium to freshen up. I applied ice cubes to my pulse spots, put my feet up, and had a cup of tea while Leila and Fatima showered and changed. I had brought no clothing with me and was beyond hope. Everything that could run had, including my makeup, which I washed off at the kitchen sink.

Abu Zaki followed us in his car to Sports City's huge auditorium. As we entered, 260 boys dressed in white shirts and black trousers donated by local merchants paraded by to take their seats on the risers at each side of the room. We sat in the first row in armchairs, next to the principal and owner of the school, who was a good friend of Leila's. She was a small, rotund woman, with thick glasses and a wide smile, wearing a headscarf and a knee-length coat. Mr. Rawabdeh, the mayor of Amman, came in and sat on the other side of the principal. I felt a tap on my shoulder. The director and the teachers from the girls' school had arrived. We all smiled a happy hello, grateful they had come as promised.

I gazed around the room. The stage was very wide and deep. Flanking its gold curtain, the purple walls held pictures of King Hussein. In front of the podium was a poster reading "Long Live King Hussein." On the stage was a plant in a brass pot, and a small table covered with a short cloth on which rested a stack of wrapped presents and underneath which sat a half-gallon bottle of water for thirsty speakers. Television cameras recorded every movement. The audience wasn't quiet; there were whistles, *lalalalas*, clapping, a constant murmur. Men and children unconcernedly climbed the stairs to the stage and walked behind the curtain in the midst of speeches.

There were many speakers. Abu Zaki or Leila translated the major themes of the program, softly whispering the words of songs or speeches to me. The first speaker loved Palestine and Jordan. He would go back to his country, and King Hussein would be the leader. Much applause. The Qur'an was quoted. Students sang without accompaniment, with long pauses between lines. Between speeches, a group of boys sang a song about Lebanon, a tambourine and drums punctuating the chorus. Tiny preschool girls in costume ran out from behind the curtain and danced. Leila had made the costumes to represent each village a few years before and had donated them to the school. Eight little girls dressed alike came out to recite a poem. They elbowed each other, trying to be the one directly in front of the microphone. One little girl, unable to squeeze in anywhere, ran back and forth from one end of the line to the other. The audience laughed and clapped. Seventeen little girls marched across the stage, each holding aloft a red carnation in her hand for the soldiers who had died for Palestine, while boys asked the world to allow them to return to their country and gave the birds who flew over their villages their best wishes. Two tiny girls, orphans from another society started by the principal, came out to dance, bodies swaying, feet moving on tiptoe, arms weaving. There were more traditional dances by boys in costume, with singing and accompaniment by flutes and tambourines. The final impassioned speech, by the outstanding graduate of the class, "Are You an Arab?" rang out.

"When the bell rings, all Arabs must join together and cross the river to the West Bank. I am an Arab. I call, I scream, I shout for all Arabs to unite. Are you an Arab? When the bell rings, will you join? You people who are dancing and spinning, put your hands together. We go to my house, my country, my people."

There were sobs and then much clapping.

A mock trial began. A trio of Palestinian boys dressed as commandos stood before a panel of Zionist "judges." They had thrown stones at Zionists. Three boys dressed as Israeli soldiers pretended to strike one commando with rifles. He collapsed. A witness for the Israelis testified. Drums rolled, the commando shrieked his response to the witness's testimony. The audience whistled and clapped.

"You are from Russia, Germany, Poland. What are you doing in our country? Who gives you the right to keep us in jail until we die? We will still go back to our country."

Small girls from the audience rushed to the stage to dance to the song that followed.

Then the parade of graduates began. They wore no ties or jackets, and the clothes were either too big or too small for many of them. The top fifty graduates were given donated watches, presented by the mayor. After diplomas were handed out, the mayor was given the brass urn and tray, which had been sitting on the stage, as a gift for his help.

It was evening when we left the auditorium. Fatima was taken home by Abu Zaki, but the day wasn't yet over for us. Leila and I picked up my husband, stopped at a bakery for sweets, and went to the apartment of Bassam, who had graduated that day and whose family was to receive the clothing Leila had put in her car that morning. Bassam was the son of Omar, a man whose health and spirit had been broken at thirty-four. Leila and Abu Zaki had supported Bassam through high school, knowing that upon completion of college he would begin to support his family.

It was the first time Leila had taken us to a poor residential area within the city of Amman. The buildings were multistoried, each housing many families. The roads were pocked with deep holes and ruts. We parked on a rise, and then carefully picked our way through pitch blackness to a doorway only Leila could see. The others had better night vision than I and were far ahead of me. When I arrived at the doorway, there was no sign of anyone. I was alone, wandering up and down the open cement staircases, hoping to hear a familiar voice. Since there were no handrails, I could only feel my way toward thin streams of light coming from under the doors. While I knew that no one would harm me, my mind kept flashing pictures of the plight of outsiders who invaded the protected turf of ghettos in my own country. I panicked and began banging on the doors, shouting for someone to answer. When they did, I asked for Omar. They would shrug and close their doors. At last I heard someone calling out to me. They had finally realized I wasn't with them.

"Keep calling until I find you," I cried, feeling my way along the walls as I carefully descended each step. "I can't see where you are."

"Pat, why were you not with us?" Leila was solicitous.

"I was moving too slowly, Leila. I'll keep up with you next time, believe me." I laughed nervously. I couldn't let her know I had been scared to death. She ushered me into the living/sleeping area to meet the large family. Lee already had a child on his knee. I was welcomed and sat with Lee on one of the two daybeds while Leila talked with Nijmeh, Bassam's mother, and some of the children. Bassam and Omar were out. The girls busied themselves making tea in the little room nearby that served for cooking and, I guessed, for sleeping.

There were shouts of greeting as Bassam entered. When I saw his father, I reeled back in shock. He weighed no more than eighty pounds, his skin stretched so tightly across his skeletal face that his lips were in a perpetual grimace. Several teeth were missing or broken. He seemed nervous and distant, not wanting to sit with us—as if he would take up too much space. We convinced him to join us, and some of the children moved off the daybed onto the floor to make room for him.

While cakes and tea were being served, Bassam told us how pleased he was that we had witnessed his special day, and about his plans for university. The children spoke good English, and we were able to learn about the education system and the aspirations of graduates who passed the certificate exam, which Bassam was to take a month hence. As we talked, I glanced occasionally at Omar, whose eyes remained downcast and whose thin arms rested on his knees, barely supporting him. Bassam's mother also looked defeated and worn, although her eyes shone with pride for her son.

When we had finished our tea and cakes, Leila sent some of the children to the car for the bags of clothing. When they had gone, she asked Bassam to speak with us about his father. Bassam spoke with Omar in Arabic for a moment and then began.

"My father says I may tell you about him and our family.

"I am eighteen, the first son. I have two brothers and five sisters. Since early childhood, we have suffered psychologically because of the abuses to our father and mother.

"My father was detained by the Israeli authorities three times: for eight months in 1968, for almost three years in 1970, and for five months in 1976. Then he was deported to Amman. The consequences of the last detention were appalling. We observed with deep sorrow the excruciating pain inflicted upon our father while he was in prison. We saw him dwindle to a skeleton of skin and bones, dropping to half his weight. Fractures of his skull, jaw, and nearly all his ribs dropped him into hallucinations and a coma. He was on the verge of death.

"The Red Cross tried to save my father by transferring him from an Israeli prison to an Amman hospital. This was ultimately achieved in February of 1977, when he crossed the Allenby Bridge over the Jordan River on a stretcher.

"The *Sunday Times* of London published an article on June 19, 1977, giving details of the atrocities inflicted on some of the detainees. One of them was my father. I have a copy of the article, which I will give you to read. The article came to the attention of President Carter, who inquired of the Prime Minister the detainees' condition.

"We were removed to Amman to be beside our father, because he was not expected to live. I started school and progressed steadily, but moderately. The condition of my father is a constant strain of body and mind. In spite of treatment, his condition worsens. I must succeed. With my education, I will be able to help my family."

Bassam's fervent words were accompanied by movement to obtain the copy of the article about his father. As he pressed it into my hand I asked about his mother. Leila, Lee, and the children sat utterly still, listening intently.

"How did your mother care for all of you while your father was in prison?"

"I will ask my mother your questions and translate her answers to you."

"Please ask her to start at the beginning, Bassam."

Nijmeh explained, "I am descended from a Palestinian family, originally from the village of Sataf, north of Jerusalem. My father and his new wife, with both their families, were expelled from Sataf during the War of 1948. They settled in Beit Sahur, south of Bethlehem. I was born there the next year.

"My husband, Omar, was born in Sataf in 1942 and moved with his family to Beit Sahur in 1948. He finished his secondary education in 1958 and began a two-year vocational training program in carpentry. Meanwhile, I was growing into a young woman, with rosy cheeks, a fair complexion, and fine stature. My name means 'star.' When Omar asked for my hand, he told me I twinkled and glowed brighter than the stars in the sky. We were married in 1964. Omar proved to be a very skillful carpenter, was hired by Bandak's establishment, and was making a good income.

"We were living comfortably and happily with our first son, Bassam, who was born in 1965, and our daughter Thuraya, who was born in 1967. Then came the 1967 War and the occupation of the West Bank by Israel. Since that time, our lives have become a chain of hardship and misery. Omar was imprisoned for eight months after the occupation. He was suspected of being a PLO sympathizer. Our second daughter, Amani, was born in 1968 while he was still in prison. When Omar was released, we thought he could resume carpentry and again stand on his own feet. Another daughter was born in 1969.

"In 1970, our lives were again interrupted. Omar was again imprisoned, this time for almost three years. He was subjected to such incredible torture that he required six months of hospitalization in Israeli hospitals. We were in despair. We had no income. To survive, our grandfather gave us some help, and I made pastry and sweets, which Bassam sold.

"On Omar's release, he found no vacancies in carpentry work and decided to start a private business. With his deteriorating health and his shattered body, he made very little progress. During this period, our second and third sons were born.

"Once again, now for the third time, Omar was imprisoned. It was 1976, we had six children, and the family was in desperate financial straits. Bassam again sold the pastries, biscuits, and sweets I prepared at home. He continues to sell them to this day. It was all we could do to survive. Then, six weeks before Omar's release, I was imprisoned. I was taken before Omar and beaten in his presence to force a confession from me. I had nothing to confess. Omar was completely exhausted. I could see the marks of beatings he had endured. He 'confessed' to save me. He had done nothing. Secretly, the Red Cross reported the atrocities inflicted on my husband. The London *Sunday Times* investigated and confirmed the tortures he received. Later, President Carter asked Prime Minister Begin about the torture of Palestinian prisoners, and specifically mentioned the debilitated state of Omar. It was then that Israel deported Omar—before he died on them. The Red Cross mediated his transfer to Amman on humanitarian reasons.

"I was released two weeks before Omar's deportation and was permitted to come to Amman to meet my husband on the bridge. On that day, I was as if struck by a bolt of lightning. Omar was just a skeleton, with a vacant, fixed gaze, gasping for breath, and unaware of anything or anyone around him. I directed the ambulance to take us to the nearest hospital, which was in Salt. The children joined us. Later, we transferred him to Hussein Medical Center in Amman, so we could visit often. After four months of dedicated treatment, he was unable to regain even a part of his health, so he was released to convalesce at home. To this day, there is no noticeable improvement. He constantly complains of pains and aches all over his body, and all we have to give him is aspirin.

"When Umm Zaki read Omar's story in the newspapers, she visited us and was deeply touched by Omar's deplorable condition. Now, thanks to the little income from the sale of my sweets and the continuous help of Abu Zaki and Umm Zaki, we can survive."

Some of the children, who had been sorting the bags of clothing, rejoined the rest of us.

"Bassam, tell your mother I thank her very much for telling us her story. Lee and I are privileged to meet her and your father and all the members of your family. And I had the additional privilege of witnessing your graduation. What a proud day this must be for her and your father. And for you!"

All the family agreed they were proud and happy for their son and brother. He would begin studying immediately for the entrance examinations to university.

When we left Omar and Nijmeh and their family late that night, we could hear children crying and families talking through the thin walls that separated the apartments. As the car bounced over the rocks and potholes to a paved street, Leila urged me to read the article Bassam had given me.[1]

We had seen slum living at its worst. Yet, thanks to Leila and her husband, another family had survived. Their son had achieved. Another small stone would make a thousand ripples. Unfortunately, this stone would not be thrown as quickly as all of us had hoped. The strain and pressure finally took its toll. Bassam failed his examinations. Psychological treatment has begun, and Bassam will retake the examinations when he is well.

1998 – Bassam passed his examinations and then received a degree in heating and air conditioning in the U.S.S.R., married a Russian colleague and has two sons. Omar became weaker and was diagnosed with tuberculosis. The terrible pain he suffered began to lessen. Their second son is in poor health, the third a blacksmith. Their daughters graduated and married.

CHAPTER SEVEN

It's the Same as if You Put in a Carbon

My husband's only day off was Friday, in keeping with the religious day of the Muslims. We usually spent that day with members of the Friends of Archaeology Society, visiting digs or ancient ruins, or exploring on our own the wonders of Jordan. I preferred to spend most of the remaining six days with Leila. If she called at the last minute, I revised my plans to accommodate hers. Lee left for work at eight each morning, and I would meet Leila at the curb a few minutes later, and our day would begin. This particular day began with one of those last-minute calls.

"Pat, please change your plan for today. We must go instead to Baqa'a. There is a problem."

Early as it was, I was waiting. Leila seemed too preoccupied to talk. As we raced toward Baqa'a, we passed a new construction site. She slammed on the brakes and backed the car down the middle of the two-lane highway, oblivious of the angry motorists on either side of us. One of the construction workers motioned to her to stop honking, and when he got no response, he stormed up to the car. They spoke hurriedly in Arabic, and the worker motioned the driver of the loader to come. Still sitting in the middle of the highway, traffic halted, horns blaring, the three of them held an animated conversation. We pulled away, Leila calling goodbyes as if she were the only person on the road.

"Others look for dresses. I look for loaders." Then, "They put Mustafa in jail because he protected the sanitation center."

"In jail? Oh my God, Leila. What can we do?"

"We are going to see him now. They have released him. He is angry. We must tell him we have found a loader."

"Leila, I don't understand this problem! Mustafa going to jail, you hiring loaders in the middle of the highway! Why would Mustafa have to protect the center? Did someone want to tear it down after all your work?"

"Thanks to God it isn't that bad. No one is tearing down our work. The problem, Pat, is that the loader hired from the municipality by UNRWA sometimes does not come to Baqa'a. It is supposed to come every day. Mustafa's house is at one of the eleven collection points in the camp. When the loader doesn't come, the garbage gets higher and higher. Why? Because the rubbish men employed by UNRWA keep hauling wheelbarrows of garbage they pick up on the way to the collection points. Mustafa became angry with the rubbish man. After all, could he not see that the garbage was getting higher? Yet he kept on dumping more and more garbage. Mustafa stopped him. The rubbish man reported him to the manager of the camp. The manager sent for the police and they put him in jail for stopping the man from doing his work."

We pulled up at a school building close to the camp entrance. Mustafa had chosen to meet us there to avoid the time-consuming slowing and stopping for pedestrian traffic. He jumped into the car before I could get out to hold the seat up for him. His face was set, his eyes were blazing, and his voice trembled with anger.

"I knew trying to solve our situation was only a dream. For sixteen years, we begged. Nothing was done. What could we do? Then we solved it. The children are playing. The ladies are sitting around the playground.

It is clean. The people are proud of their work. They want to make it go. Now we have no loader come, and the problem is just as bad as before. Sixteen years. Nothing has changed."

His arms rested on his knees, his head drooping dispiritedly.

"You come to help us, Umm Zaki. The poor people love you very much. They think, *Only Umm Zaki helps us*. For ten years, people have come to visit me telling stories of problems. My friends say, 'If you have a problem with UNRWA or anyone, Umm Zaki has the answer.' What is the answer now, Umm Zaki?"

"Mustafa, I've offered a man six dinars to bring his loader. I will go to UNRWA and tell them a man has been paid to come. The loader will take all the trash it can carry. The rubbish man can come and dump new wheelbarrows full of trash. In this way, all will be happy. The rubbish man will have his work, and UNRWA will not have a problem from Mustafa. I will go to see the mayor of the municipality to find out why the loader isn't coming here."

Mustafa straightened up. His smile was blinding. Hope replaced helplessness. "Come," he offered expansively, "we will go to my house. We will talk."

He had been accurate in his description. The garbage heap was higher than a two-story building and shut out the sunlight from the doorways surrounding it. The smell was so overpowering that I took off my headscarf and buried my face in it. Mustafa apologized as we carefully picked our way to his doorway.

Over the door hung a framed passage from the Qur'an. Strewn on the floor inside were five straw mats, on one of which lay a sleeping baby, wrapped tightly in a crocheted blanket. Several women were sewing, and they smiled and spoke to us as we came in. Two small carpets hung on the wall, one of them depicting the three Wise Men looking at Jesus in the manger. On the other, two peacocks stood on a balcony ledge overlooking a field of flowers, with a lake and castle in the distance. The pictures provided the only color in the room. As soon as we were settled down, Mustafa took out his precious diary, tattered and ragged from many years of use. Assured that he had my attention, he began to read from it.

"There were five of us children. We had no parents. My father died when I was two, my mother died when I was five. There were many misunderstandings in our family about us children, and we paid for it. We were shifted from relative to relative. We stayed with an aunt in Baqa'a. She had thirteen people in her room; with us, it became eighteen. When there was a family quarrel, we would be taken from Baqa'a and sent to Marka to my grandfather, or to Hussein Camp with other relatives, and then back to Baqa'a. My brothers and sister left school for a while because of transportation problems. I stayed in school and studied hard day and night. I was always first in class.

"Finally, an uncle returned from Libya and took us to Baqa'a to stay. We lived with him until 1980. My brothers have married, so I share a room now in my uncle's house.

"I was nine years old when the Israelis came in 1967. Thousands of people fled. We had no weapons, as it was against the law to have them. Our relatives fled with us children from Ramallah to Jericho, near the Dead Sea, then to Salt in Jordan. We spent two months in a school in Amman, and lived fifteen persons to a room. Then we were transferred to Souf Camp near Jerash and lived in a tent. After one and a half months, the sky was raining so much the water came up from the ground. People died.

I had a friend who was also nine. He lived with strangers for one month, looking for his parents. Finally, he found his mother in a food line. He was so happy. But when it rained so hard and the camp was washed away, his mother, sister, and two brothers died.

"The police came and took us from Souf by bus to a camp in Zezia near

Alia Airport, south of Amman. Tents were put up in the night. There was no cover on the ground, just dirt. The police surrounded us and forbade the people to leave the camp. It was very cold. For three days there was no food, no water, nothing. The police caught my uncle leaving the camp to find ground cover to protect us and put him in prison for two days. When he came back, he told my aunt to leave everything; they would go from this place in the night. We walked for three days. The police found us and took us back.

"We started walking again to go back to Palestine. We got as far as King Hussein Bridge and remained there for one month. Then the Israelis came and damaged the camp. We had to leave. It took us ten days to walk to Amman. We lived in the streets, asking daily about another camp. They told us they had built a new camp, Baqa'a.

"Baqa'a Camp was built after the 1967 War, in February 1968. There was no work for three years; no schools, nothing for a while. What shall we do sitting behind the tents? Groups formed. We started quarreling. There were so many people in the tents that some had to go out so others could sleep. Some shops opened. I needed to buy, but I had no money. I wanted to work, but there was no work. I decided I would shine shoes, but after a week I saw no one had shoes. My uncle bought a newspaper and sent me to the tea shops, where the men talked and smoked. Seven men paid one piaster each to read the paper. I had a job! Then many men started renting papers at the shops. I was eleven and out of work again. My aunt made sweets to sell. No one bought. All the children were doing the same thing. I changed jobs. I went to the food center, where they threw away cartons. I collected them, put metal bottoms on them and sold them for shoes. Soon there wasn't a box in the camp. Everyone was doing the same thing. A man suggested I get plastic shoes and sell them. Where could I get them? I had no money to buy them. On Fridays all the people prayed in the mosque and left their shoes outside. I collected the shoes and sold them. The next Friday everyone carried their shoes under their arms when they went in to pray. I was out of a job again!

"People wanted to eat. Because of trouble with giving food from trucks, UNRWA made a food center. Only one member of the family could stand in line when the truck came. All the men and women had to go to the food center. The police came every day and beat the people because they were not standing in line. Some had been standing for three hours, others for three days. The police, instead of throwing one troublemaker out of line, threw everyone out and commanded them to make a new line. The women were crying. UNRWA employees used shovels to throw the food from the window of the center. It hit the people. Everyone tried to catch it. Fights started. For three years it went on like this.

"There was one latrine for 3,000 people. When it was full, it was covered with sand. People waited all day until the sun went down to evacuate their waste. They used a piece of paper as an envelope for the waste and threw the envelope as far as they could. It landed on tents. The people in the tents became angry. Fighting started.

"As people got work, conditions changed. Trucks brought tanks of water. People stood in line. They filled one container for each family for cleaning, drinking, and washing the clothes. When I was older, I cleaned cars, drove taxis, and did construction work.

"It went on like this until I was fifteen. I had been running and moving for six years, but I was good in school. It was arranged for me to go to school in Kuwait on a scholarship. I spent five years there, finishing technical college in chemistry. After working for two years, I went to Iraq and got my engineering degree. Others had mothers and fathers who were afraid for them to go away. I had no one to say, 'Don't go,' so I went.

"A cement factory hired me when I came back. I was twenty-four. I want to buy a house and a car, and get married. I am earning 250 dinars a month. Eighty to ninety dinars is average; fifty to sixty is low. It will take years to earn enough money for a house, and I can buy a car only if my brothers buy it with me and we share it with the family. When a house is bought, the owner keeps it or rents it out. In 1979, we began paying 150 dinars a month for renting a house; we have ninety-six square meters. It will cost 4,500 to 5,000 dinars to buy the house. A truck comes to remove the sewage water from the cesspool every six days; that costs thirty dinars a month. It is fourteen dinars for drinking water and ten dinars for electricity. From what is left we must buy clothes, medicine, food, and fuel. How can we live?

"There is no progress here. It is the same as if you put in a carbon. Everything that was built for three must now do for twelve or twenty. We have the same land with two rooms. Only rarely does it change for a family. We have had electricity in the camps for only two or three years. It came to our section only this year.

"I can't see my uncle work at his age. All of us boys work to support him. Two teach, one is an architect, and I am an engineer of unit operations. When my father was alive, he owned trucks for his two quarries and his two brick factories; he was very rich. What happened to all the money? When my father died long ago, my uncles took everything; they did not learn to run their own businesses. We children ended up in the camps. People tell me that if my father was alive, I would be rich now. Sometimes I am sorry they tell me."

Mustafa closed the diary. During his recital I had sat, legs tucked under me, without moving a muscle. Respect for Mustafa kept the others quiet, even though they spoke no English. I longed to put my arms around this angry young man, to give him the mother's comfort life had denied him, but custom forbade it. Instead I covered the hand that held the diary with mine and thanked him in Arabic.

"Shukran, Mustafa, shukran. Your deprivations have made you strong. You've grown to be a sensitive, caring, and certainly enterprising young man. Now that you and Leila have met, everything good will happen."

"It is already happening, Miss Pat. She is my friend. You are my friend."

Our eyes met and acknowledged that indeed we were friends and would be no matter how far apart we might be in the future. Leila and I shared the warmth of his words all the way home.

Later, as I read about the 1967 War, I came across much that substantiated Mustafa's story. On the morning of June 5, 1967, Israeli fighter-bombers attacked ten Egyptian air bases simultaneously, demolishing the new Egyptian Air Force in less than three hours. The Syrian and Jordanian Air Forces were destroyed by midday, and the Iraqi Air Force by the next morning. In all during those two days, 416 Arab planes had been destroyed.

At the same time, the Israeli Infantry and Armored Forces broke through the Egyptian forward positions and raced westward to trap the Egyptian Army and prevent its escape from the Sinai Desert, reaching the Suez Canal after four days, with seven decimated U.A.R. Divisions behind them.[1]

With the skillful and strategic protection of air cover, Israeli ground troops successfully overran the West Bank and the Old City of Jerusalem. By sundown on the tenth of June, Israel had captured the Syrian highlands and the Golan Heights, containing the eastern part of the watershed sources of the Jordan River, an area that Chaim Weizmann had long before urged be incorporated into Palestine for the Jewish national home. In a mere six days, the Israelis found themselves securely positioned in their newly conquered territories after accepting the U.N. demand for a ceasefire.[2]

After the ceasefire, Israel blocked Red Cross efforts to rescue soldiers who lay wounded and dying in the desert. By June 19, the daily count of sunburned and blistered survivors of the Egyptian Sinai forces struggling to reach the Canal was fast approaching zero. The Israeli Army estimated 40,000 Egyptian and Jordanian casualties. By comparison, only 679 Israeli soldiers died in the siege. On November 22, 1967, the U.N. Security Council passed Resolution 242, ordering Israeli withdrawal from the occupied territories and Arab renouncement of belligerence and recognition of Israel within secure frontiers.[3] The formula was flawed by one ambiguity, however, in that it failed to define clearly the perimeters of the occupied territory from which Israel was to withdraw. The omission of the word "all" in terms of the occupied territory became a critical issue and still remains a bone of contention. The Arabs maintain that the text implies Israeli withdrawal from *all* occupied territory, while the Israelis insist that it provides for their retention of some of it.[4]

The Arabs rejected Resolution 242 because of its implication that Israel be recognized as a state and referred only to "refugees" rather than the Palestinian people. The Israelis also rejected Resolution 242 and refused to withdraw from the occupied territory because it wanted to enter a peace treaty with the Arab countries without U.N. mediation, demanding face-to-face negotiations with the Arabs. Resolution 242 also failed because Israel had no intention of withdrawing from Jerusalem, which it has claimed as its capital since 1967, although it has never been acknowledged as such by other nations, who, with the exception of El Salvador and South Africa, continue to keep their embassies in Tel Aviv.[5]

The deliberate damage done to the camp at the Damia Bridge—as well as to the King Hussein Bridge and other shelters—in December (long after the ceasefire) that Mustafa told me about was described by Henry Cattan in his book, *Palestine, the Arabs and Israel*, as follows:

> On December 2, 1967, some 800 houses and refugee shelters in the Jordan Valley near the Damia Bridge on the Jordan River, which were inhabited by 6,000 people, mostly refugees, were wiped out by bulldozers of the Israeli Army. The official explanation was that "the area was infested with rats which threatened the health

of Israeli soldiers in a military post in the neighbourhood." On December 8, 1967, UNRWA lodged a protest to the Government of Israel against the systematic destruction of refugee houses and shelters. The destruction of Arab homes was also condemned on March 8, 1968, by the United Nations Commission on Human Rights which called upon Israel "to desist forthwith from acts of destroying homes of the Arab civilian population inhabiting areas occupied by Israel"".... The destruction of houses or other property by a military occupier is contrary to international law and is forbidden by the Geneva Conventions of 1949. The second refugee tragedy displaced a further 410,248 Palestinians from the West Bank and the Gaza Strip, according to estimates by the Government of Jordan on May 31, 1968. Their figure includes 145,000 Palestinian refugees from the 1948 War who had been registered with UNRWA before and were again displaced in June 1967, plus 180,000 new refugees from the West Bank and Gaza. Add 16,000 registered with UNRWA as refugees from 1948 who had been displaced in Syria, as well as 3,000 to 4,000 expelled by Israel from the Gaza Strip to Egypt. Another 100,000 were displaced from the occupied areas in Syria, 60,000 to 70,000 from the Sinai Peninsula, and about 300,000 from the Suez Canal Zone as a result of Israeli bombardments. At a meeting of the Special Political Committee of the United Nations on December 14, 1967, Israel's representative referred to this displacement as "a free and orderly migration."[6]

Such was the description given of this appalling human tragedy, this second exodus from Palestine.

CHAPTER EIGHT

I Can Make a Contribution, Can't I?

ALL THAT REMAINED TO COMPLETE THE SANITATION center was the lighting. At the end of one busy day, we stopped at the humble office of the one private physician in Baqa'a Camp. After discussing delivery of the necessary items, Leila asked him to tell me about his practice. He invited us in to sit down on one of the two wooden benches in the unadorned waiting area, and began.

"My name is Nabil. I live in Amman and maintain my clinic here. I served as a government doctor for my two years of military duty. I didn't know much about the camps and thought of working with UNRWA. They suggested Baqa'a. There was no private doctor in the camp, so I felt I could make a contribution. After seeing the situation, I decided that instead of working with UNRWA, I would have a private clinic, where I might serve in a better way. I have been with this for twelve years, and there has never been a private doctor other than me. Private doctors serve only 15 percent of the population; government, UNRWA, and military doctors serve the remaining 85 percent. There is a shortage of doctors.

"There are at least 80,000 people here, if not more. Some can pay; some cannot. Others come from societies or associations in their villages who inform us how many poor people they have, then send the people through the society for free or for half-cost. Every city has an organization formed by the rich people. They classify the people from their city and give them a card. Certain doctors, hospitals, and pharmacies serve the poor for free. When the person shows a white card, he pays some; when he shows a green card, he pays nothing.

"I am a general practitioner. I see everything. The economic status here is very low. Sixty percent of the diseases result from living conditions. Psychological disorders are also common. For instance, a young woman can't solve a problem. She says she is ill. She is living with her father in one room. The father, a widower, wants to remarry. He cannot have another room, only a curtain. The girl is fifteen. She can't stay; she can't go.

"Perhaps 1 percent of the people in the camps are rich. If they have money, they usually don't stay here. They live outside. If they stay, their entire family, brothers and their wives and children, etc., usually live in the home.

"The refugees pay no taxes, and many pay no rent. If they were to pay for those two items, how would they eat? They cannot afford nourishing food. That's why there is so much malnutrition in the camp. Think of these poor people trying to create a meal for as many as sixteen people. They have meat once a week or once a month, sometimes eggs, mostly rice. It isn't nourishing. They don't grow well. The children play in the streets, so there are many accidents, or they play in the garbage. They hit each other, quarrel. What else is there to do? There are kerosene and medicine poisonings, burns. The most prevalent diseases are diarrhea, trachoma, meningitis, mumps, fungal infections where the hair falls out, chicken pox, worms, measles, rubella, polio, and chest infections. Before school, from four months to six years, gastroenteritis is most common.

"There are many maternal deaths in childbirth. Unqualified midwives use the dirtiest implements, instead of the cleanest, so they can throw them away after birth. There is much anemia and late bleeding. Child mortality is high. I tried to make a midwifery center here, but was not allowed to do it. The reason given me was that the hospital is only thirty minutes away by car. These people can't afford to pay fifty dinars to have a child delivered in the hospital. The midwife charges only five to ten dinars.

"Patients go to the hospital in trucks or taxis. At Karak, one patient had her baby on the tractor they were driving to the hospital, so they took her back home. The women are nervous because of the number of children they have. Their husbands are working all day outside, so the burden is on the women. But birth control is not an acceptable alternative. For some it is against their religion; for others it's because of national feelings. Their attitude is 'We must compensate for the losses. They are trying to finish us off as a nation. We are not going to die. This is our duty.' Husbands come to me to ask me to convince the women not to bear children, but not the wives. Twenty percent of the men might have two wives. Maybe the first wife can have no children and doesn't want divorce as remarriage is difficult for a barren woman. The first wife helps to find the second wife, usually her friend. The first wife is now safe from divorce, which makes her happy and willing to care for the second wife's children sometimes better than the second wife cares for them.

"UNRWA assistance falls far short of the needs of the refugees. Doctors are limited in number, and there is no patient education. They don't give the patients the reasons for their illness or tell them what is right or wrong. A doctor sees 120 patients in six and a half hours. That's one patient every three minutes. They ask, 'What is your illness?' and then write a prescription without even looking up. What they need is all the facilities in well-equipped clinics. But there are budget restrictions. One hospital in Jerash serves Baqa'a as well as two other camps. There are only a few subsidized beds.

"A private dentist works with me. He is trying to teach the people to save their teeth. The UNRWA dentist is here on Saturdays and Tuesdays. The rest of his days are spent in other camps. He does one or two fillings a day and ten to fifteen extractions. Most teeth cannot be saved by the time he gets to them.

"My nurse has her secondary certificate in practical nursing. I also hire a couple of boys, twelve to fourteen years old, to clean the offices. It gives the family money.

"My father has money. He gave me my house and my car. I buy nothing for my house. I am here to serve my people. I average thirty to forty patients a day. I work twelve hours a day, six days a week, but the trouble is they come to me only when they lose confidence in UNRWA. People with money come to me from the very beginning. Others can come the first time without money, but they don't. I am 75 percent successful in treating my patients. When it is too complicated, I send them to private or government hospitals, and doctors there are willing to serve. Those who will help with lab investigations and X-rays are already well known to us.

"When Umm Zaki comes to me for help, I always try to help her. I want to help all my patients, but it's impossible. Without proper sanitation, they will never be really well. Umm Zaki's work is the key to improving their health. When the garbage dumps are removed, and when the sewage no longer runs in the streets, these children will have a chance to grow to school age."

The refugees had told me similar stories. I hadn't wanted to believe that such callousness existed, but Nabil corroborated what Mustafa had said about life in the camps today being "just like a carbon" of the beginning: that UNRWA doctors didn't examine the patients, that they didn't look up from the table when the patient stood before them describing his illness, and that no matter how severe the problem, the major prescription was aspirin.

"Leila, if he's working twelve hours a day and six out of ten people come to him for treatment of illnesses caused by living in the camp, more than half of his work is for nothing!"

"I know. That is why we must change these things. We have removed one garbage dump. It is a small step. More steps will follow. One day all the dumps will be gone. Children will not be poisoned or burned or crippled. We will have fewer orphans. Remember when I told you about the orphanage in Wadi-al-seer? Queen Alia had died in a plane crash just before I went to see His Majesty. I told His Majesty, 'The Ministry of Social Welfare needs a mother, not a father. Her Majesty is gone only forty days. Your children have no mother. You have two orphans. But these children have no father, no mother, no food, no nothing.' The problem of the orphans was shown on television. The King ordered all concerned to work hard to improve the condition of the orphans.

"We must make friends. People will see we are a generous, hospitable people. That we are trying. Then perhaps they will help just as King Hussein helped us."

CHAPTER NINE

The Helpless Become the Helpful

IT WAS A DAY WHEN THE WEATHER SEEMED A LITTLE hotter, the traffic a little heavier, the refugees a little more despondent, and their stories a little more painful and a little less solvable. For the first time, I heard frustration in Leila's voice. I recalled asking her once if she ever lost her temper, and she had replied that she became angry only when her car broke down. So I suggested something a bit more heartening. "There's so much despair and heartache," I told her. "I sure could use a little lift. Don't any of the people you've helped ever reciprocate with their own help to others?"

Leila responded to this in her usual style. After finishing that day's work we went to Hussein Camp to visit some widows with *happy* stories to tell. On the way we shared stories about our own children. Her son Zaki had just returned to Jordan from an engineering assignment. Monia had just given birth to twins, the second son Amjad was studying at university, and Maysoon had graduated in landscape design and was living at home—a lovely, wholesome, sharing family. My oldest daughter was studying veterinary medicine, my middle daughter was a new mother, and my son, a Navy pilot, was in Japan. Lee's only child, a son, was in insurance and lived with his family in Wisconsin. Thus, in this mutual warmth we arrived at the camp and were welcomed by Rahila and her family.

As we entered their home, I noticed the floor was the usual cement, one light tube hung from the ceiling, and a tiny, high window let in a little natural light. The furniture in the room we were in was limited to a narrow daybed with a floral cover. Against one wall were the usual metal wardrobes on legs, one with a plastic faux-marble front, the other with a sheet hanging in front of it. The bedding and clothing were stored neatly. The only other item in the room was an open cabinet on which sat a small television set.

About five feet tall, extremely thin, with dark eyes and olive skin, Rahila began her story.

"I was born in a cave during the 1948 War while my family was fleeing to safety. I married at fourteen because we had no food at home. My husband died and left me with one child. A year later, I married my second husband, but after six years he died in an accident. I was two months pregnant. My children are thirteen, eleven, nine, seven, and four-year-old twins. I was living in the street, but now I live here with my mother. Someone told Umm Zaki about me."

At this point, Leila picked up on the story. "I began caring for her and the children five years ago. I found out she had twins and started to send her things. But she was so sick, I sent her to the hospital, where they found she had a tumor in her kidney. She is still sick but we are praying for God to give her health to raise her children. Her tumor requires seven kinds of medicine. She cannot go into the shops or the street because she falls down and must be carried back to the house."

Then Rahila's mother, her hair hennaed bright red, came into the room holding one of the twins, who was sick with the measles. She came over to me and kissed the top of my head. I asked her to tell me how she had come to the camp.

"I am from the village of Haditha in Lydda. My whole family was living there. My husband built houses, and I planted the land. We had one boy and four girls. The boy was the oldest. My husband built us a house with three rooms and a big sitting room for the family. One morning in 1948 we saw an airplane over our houses throwing papers that said 'Leave your country immediately or we will kill you. If you don't leave, we will bomb you.' I was full-term pregnant. Rahila was born while we were running. I hid in a cave and gave birth to Rahila all by myself, without the help of a midwife. Thank God I didn't bleed to death. When we reached Qybia, we hid. We saw the Israelis come and kill the villagers.

"We ran to the caves. The people there said they were killing our people with knives, so we fled to Abud, then to Umm Safa to collect olives to live, and then on to Ramallah. We could get flour and milk there, so we stayed for one year. Then we heard the Israelis were coming to Ramallah, and we were afraid the same thing would happen as before, so we fled to Amman.

"When we arrived, we found the area all prepared for us. UNRWA gave us a tent. We lived here in the tent for eleven years. The poor conditions have given my son, who is now forty, chronic bronchitis, and my daughter, who is thirty-eight, a rheumatic heart. Now, Rahila has a tumor in her kidney. When we fled from our house, there were five children. Now Rahila has six, one daughter has twelve, and my boy has two wives and twenty-four children. The original seven have become forty-six!

"In the camp, the families each took twelve kilos of flour, one kilo of sugar, one can of oil, and four pieces of soap. We have remained here since, and all my children grew up here. When my daughter's husband died, there was no place for her to live. Umm Zaki found out about her and came to me. She said if I would let my daughter live with me, she would care for us. Umm Zaki built us a kitchen and sent the children to the school for orphans.

"I think often of our land—we owned twenty-five dunums. My

husband built around Beir Nabala and Dair Tarif. He walked each way. When the Israelis came in 1948, I was thirty and my husband was forty years old. One of my brothers left with us, but he was killed on the way to Qybia.

"I cannot work because of disc problems that came from running when I was nine months pregnant, and Rahila can't work because of the tumor. She goes to the hospital as a charity patient. My husband died from high blood pressure and a heart attack. I take heart pain medicine."

When Leila explained that she took them the help they needed each month, including donated clothes, I asked her, "How can people give and give when each donation is small compared to the size of the problem?"

"Even if Palestinians say UNRWA cares for our people, in their hearts they feel they themselves are responsible. They are one with each other. When I call on Palestinians for help, they never refuse. Even toys are donated. Rahila needs a house. That's why we're here. If anything happens to her mother, the house will be sold for perhaps 2,000 dinars. This house was for her mother and father. There are four daughters and one boy. If the mother dies, the house will be split five ways. Each child will receive one-fifth of the sale price. So what will Rahila do then? She will have no place to live. We must build her a house. Social welfare will give her a small piece of land, probably at another camp."

"Why don't they just buy the land they have now and expand it as they get more money?"

"It's impossible. UNRWA rented the land from one man for ninety-nine years. The Hussein Camp land was not donated by the government. Everyone has about ten square meters. They have lived here for thirty-five years. Mothers and fathers can sell it, but after ninety-nine years all the land will go back to the original owner."

Leila gave Rahila a letter to take to the minister of social welfare to get the land, telling her she would get donations for construction.

When I asked Rahila to tell me about the happiest day in her life, her face lit up, and with a beatific smile she said, "The day Umm Zaki visited me for the first time. My name means 'never resting,' 'always on the move.' Now I can stop moving. Umm Zaki sent me to the Society for Orphans she established. They taught me to work on a treadle machine, and I obtained my certificate for sewing dresses. But I had to stop sewing at the Society because of the pain in my kidneys when I moved the treadle. Umm Zaki has found me an electric machine. As my health permits, I sew dresses for the Society."

When we left the house, Leila stopped at a small shop and bought a carton of eggs to be sent back with a child. On the way to the next stop, she reminded me of the old woman's words.

"Did you hear her say she lived in this camp for thirty-five years? Your country has spent thirty-five years giving just money to the refugees. Did you ever go to see what happens to these people?" Her voice rose. "Your money makes them worse than before! You are the most important country in the world. What did you give for thirty-five years to all these people? Just throw them food like animals? Is that all you can do? Is that where you are satisfied to see your money go? What do you know about the millions of dollars you send? Nothing. As if you throw them into the sea. No sewers to take care of the sewage in the camps. No garbage centers. How do you accept this?"

"What can I say, Leila, but that I agree with you? Until we met, I'd never heard of UNRWA. It was only when I read their brochures that I learned we are the biggest contributor. I don't know who comes from the States to see how we are spending this money, but when I get home, I'm asking."

Leila stopped short and apologized. "Oh, Pat, I am sounding like you are to blame. UNRWA respects me. I get an appointment whenever I ask. The Arab community is responsible for their people. It is with them

I am angry. No one talks about the people because they consider that the Palestine calamity is the responsibility of the United Nations, which is not enforcing its resolution on Israel. I have no position. I belong to nobody, only myself. They want me to be a director of a society, but I don't want it. If I am in a society, I talk in their name. They get afraid. I talk in my own name. If they put me in jail, I don't care."

I explained that the same problems exist in the States. "Most things are done through charitable organizations. People are happy to write a check and say, 'I gave.' The money is channeled as the organization sees fit. Donors aren't sure to what they give or to whom, but they're satisfied. Some are even smug, depending on the size of their donation. Money substitutes for involvement. Of course, we have so many more people in our country that there are more willing to help. It is said that volunteers are the backbone of American charity. Hundreds of thousands of people who cannot donate money donate time.

"Look what you do with the materials donated to you, Leila. What could you do if you had more sources of material and people were trained to help you? Under your guidance, miracles could be worked. So many talk. So few act. I'd like to act with you."

"I wish you were here for a long time, Pat."

"Me, too, Leila. Me, too." I sighed, my heart missing her already.

Then we arrived at a small, well-kept house in a residential area in Hussein Camp, parked the car, and walked up the sidewalk. The door was opened by a young girl, and we were ushered into a cool room with a large open window.

A heavyset woman with a round, gentle face, good teeth, and a generous smile sat at a Singer sewing machine with a foot pedal. She wore small, dangling gold earrings. As she sewed, I looked around the room. The floors were finished and had baseboards; the walls were painted two colors, the lower part in a glossy finish so it could be washed easily. There were separate sleeping rooms and real doors to each of the rooms instead of open entryways. Above her head was a small, wooden-framed window, kept open at night to provide ventilation to the sleeping rooms. There were screens on the outside windows.

Leila told me the woman finished dresses designed for a local charity. Because she is so talented, she gets to choose all the colors herself. Finished dress panels lay on the floor beside her, as there was no table. She was sitting on a rusty metal chair with uneven legs and no back rest. Only the corroded stretchers remained. A bare light bulb hung from the cord in the ceiling. This is what she told me.

"I am from Gaza. I cannot tell you my name because my work might be taken from me. My husband is a clerk at UNRWA and earns eighty dinars a month, but we have ten children. A neighbor told Umm Zaki to please find work for my family. When Umm Zaki first came to see me, there were no doors to any of the rooms, no windows. I told her I knew how to sew, so she sent me first to Queen Alia's mother. Umm Zaki bought me a fan so I could work comfortably in the heat, then she took me to a society and showed them my work. That was three years ago. Now I earn 150 dinars a month from my embroidery, and live peacefully.

"Two girls are still in college. When they graduate, they will work and remain at home until they marry. The others are in school. When they graduate, they will immediately go to work. I must educate my children. If anything happens to us in the future, they will care for us. If there is another war, the children will be in a better situation than we were. What is the future for our children? We want to educate them. We have no land. We came from a village and could not read or write. We saw the people who were educated. We want our children to be the same. If they are free, they will live better. When we are educated, we will go back to our country. The Israelis conquered us because they were educated.

"You were looking at my pretty dress panels on the floor. Perhaps you wonder why I don't have a table. Furniture will come one day. We can live without furniture. But we cannot live without education. Education will get us a table and chairs. A table will get us nothing."

When we left, she was threading the needle of the sewing machine she had earned, humming a little song.

1998 – Rahila remains in the camp. Her mother died. Three daughters married and left the camp. One son became an apprentice in auto mechanics. The remaining children live with their mother.

CHAPTER TEN

What Else Is There to Do But Learn?

ONE DAY, AS WE ROARED DOWN THE HIGHWAY TO Baqa'a Camp, I remembered the library.

"You know, Leila, I haven't seen the library since it was finished. Have the Arabic books arrived yet? How is the room used in the summer?"

"It is a multipurpose room. Some books have arrived and the children use it, but it's also a social center for the children and on some days for the adults."

"Could I see it in action?"

"Of course. We will see Muhammad. He's the volunteer director of the boys' activities. He will set up a time when the boys are there to show us what they do."

Muhammad's house was different from any I'd seen at Baqa'a. There was a carpet on the floor, a small cupboard with a set of dishes shimmering through its glass doors, a lamp, and a table and chairs! It was comfortable and pleasant. After we were introduced, I immediately commented on the luxuriousness of the house.

"Muhammad, please forgive me for gaping. It's just that I've never seen such a well-appointed home here."

"You see what has happened with education. We have jobs now. Things are better than ever before."

"I can see that education has helped your family immensely. I'm so happy for your success."

Tea was prepared, and after plans were made for seeing the social center, I asked Muhammad how he'd met Leila. He answered in clear, precise English, so different from the others I'd met, whose English was tentative or for whom interpretations needed to be made.

"I was head of the sports committee at the club. Leila came to the club saying there was a bad street at the south end of the camp, and the children were forced to be absent in bad weather. She asked us to bring some youths to help her repair the street. Leila was from outside the camp, but we'd heard she helped the school to make our club. We told her we'd help, but that we couldn't give money. She said she would bring materials, so we asked many to come. Leila got donations, and we got big trucks. Mustafa's uncle was one of those men. Leila tried to rent it from him, but he would take no money. He told her he'd help repair many streets any time she needed him. My mother asked Leila to call on her and took Leila to Mustafa's house. They said they needed help with their garbage and sewage problems and had received nothing for sixteen years. They asked her to help them. We've been seeing a lot of each other ever since."

We all laughed, knowing how easy it was to be caught up in Leila's transformations. After tea was served, Muhammad introduced me to his mother. He was very proud of her and wanted me to understand why. She sat with us, round and dignified, in a long, white dress rich with embroidery, her son interpreting for her.

"I was born in 1930 and was accidentally blinded in one eye when I was five. When I was six, they took my grandfather to prison. It was the law that if the English found any weapon, any pistol, in the hands of an Arab, they took him to prison. My grandfather had a knife. They put him in prison for fifteen years, but later reduced his sentence to seven years." She paused and shook her head. "For having a knife."

"I was married only seven months and was pregnant with my first baby when the Zionists attacked in 1948. We lived in the village of al-Khayriyya near Jaffa, where we owned 200 dunums of orange groves. The Mandate Army had withdrawn in 1948 from their camp near the Lydda airport. The Haganah attacked our village and killed my sister, my cousin, and my three brothers. We had no weapons—we were just citizens of the village. Our men took the women out of the village, and some young men stayed to fight with shotguns they used to kill birds. The Haganah killed everyone they saw—children, women, and men. My sister was killed because they were shooting through the windows until everyone ran out the door. Then they shot her. My sister had been engaged. They put her fiancé in prison. The terrorists were led by Menachem Begin. They conquered the villages in Palestine because no one supported the villagers. There were about 1,500 people in my village. They killed eighty-eight. The rest ran away. As the war went on, the men sold the women's gold in order to buy weapons.

"We ran. It took us days and days to reach Beit Nabala. We remained there, sleeping under olive trees, for three months late in 1948, until at last the shooting was over. We had no money and lived by bartering. Finally, we reached Ramallah, where we stayed until 1967. We lived in caves for three years, and then UNRWA gave us a tent. We began a new life.

"My husband worked as a barber and had a second job as a tenant farmer. Half the crop went to the owner. I helped with the farming and raised my children. In 1966, my oldest boy finished high school and entered UNRWA teacher-training in Ramallah. My husband is seventy-eight. He retired in 1984.

"I will tell you of Ramallah. Some of our friends died of infections, some survived them. The cave we lived in was warmer and safer than the tents provided to us. The hardest winter was in 1950, the snow year. It lasted for five months. So many died. In 1956, UNRWA built houses in Ramallah. We were settled in our new life, even though it was hard. Then in 1967 the planes came. From our place high on a mountain we could see Lydda Airport. We saw the planes attack the West Bank. Every afternoon we listened to the BBC, which gave news of both sides. All the families sat around our radio. Iraq and Jordan were standing together. The Israeli Army attacked East Jerusalem. Egypt said not to listen to the BBC, their news was wrong, but to listen only to Egypt and the Voice of America. Tanks and cars passed our camp. We thought they were Iraqi forces because the tanks looked different from Israeli tanks, so people went out to welcome them as our friends. A voice on a loudspeaker said, 'Everyone must stay inside. Do not make noise.' Jerusalem broadcast near Ramallah. Soon we heard the Voice of Amman only, and we knew Jerusalem had fallen.

"After some days, more tanks and planes came. We expected bombing and went back to the caves. When we thought it was safe, we came back to our home. The Israelis were there.

"There were many soldiers, and tanks and cars surrounded the camp. We raised white flags. Using a loudspeaker in the mosque, they told everyone to stay inside their houses. The soldiers ordered every male over sixteen to go with them. They took my husband and two of my sons to a field in the camp and asked them to show their identity cards to see if they were soldiers or citizens. Everyone with a passport was able to go back home. Those without one had to go with the soldiers. We called the *mukhtar*, the oldest man chosen by the people. The soldiers said, 'What is his job? What does he do here?' The mukhtar swore they were who they said they were, and the people without identity cards were released to go home.

"We stayed a few more days. I was very afraid because in the last dark days of 1948 I had lost my brothers. I said, 'I have sons instead of brothers now. I cannot lose my sons. We must leave.' We took what we could carry. People asked us to stay, saying we would be killed together or that there would be a solution. Thousands of others were leaving for Amman. I could not lose my sons.

"We rented a truck and drove toward the East Bank. We stopped at the Hussein Bridge, which crossed the Jordan River. At the bridge were thousands of families. The water was very deep then, and we couldn't ford the river. The Israelis had bombed the Damia and Allenby Bridges."

At this point Muhammad interjected. "All around us were abandoned and exploded Jordanian tanks. At Jericho we saw jeeps with cannons, PLO anti-tanks, bombed jeeps. They were different from those of the Jordanian Army."

Umm Muhammad continued, "It took five or six hours to cross the bridge because of the Israeli soldiers. When we reached the East Bank, we stayed some hours. My brother was working on a farm eight kilometers away. We left that night for Shunat, a few kilometers from the bridge. The Israeli armed forces attacked trucks full of people and killed them."

Again her son interrupted. "Behind one truck was a small horse cart with some people sitting on the back of the cart. I was too young to be afraid. Instead, I was curious. When we arrived at my uncle's, I left the house to see what had happened. Napalm bombs had been dropped. There was nothing but black ashes. Where the horse cart had been before, there was now an image of the horse, a few bones, and the ashes of the cart and its wheels. There were dead children, dead families everywhere."

His mother began to speak again. "We spent two days with my brother, then left for my sister's house in Amman. By then, hundreds of thousands of people were living in schools, in the mosques, on the roads. Amman was then a small town, a quarter of its present size. There were problems with water and food. But we couldn't stay in Amman, so UNRWA and the Jordanian government took us by truck and bus to Souf Camp near Jerash.

We lived there in tents for two or three months. Many insects attacked us, and food was such a problem, but at first, water wasn't, because there were many springs. About 50,000 people were living in a very small area. UNRWA gave one member of each family a card. They distributed the food according to the number of members in each family. Only the member with the card could get in line for the food truck, which came every day. It brought bread, cheese, beef, sardines, and canned goods. The lines were so long, all the families couldn't get to the truck every day. Sometimes there would be a wait of three or four days, because we would be pushed out of line.

"Finally, the Jordanian police came to maintain order. If there was any trouble from a person in line, he had to leave and go without food. Everyone hoarded what they were able to get. After two months at Souf, winter came. They took us to tents near Shunat in the Jordan Valley. There was much fighting between Jordan and Israel, and we were between them. There were bombs over our heads every day. Many children died. When they came home from school, every family dug a hole in the ground to hide from the bombs. It was said we were digging our graves, because every day and every night people died.

"We became so afraid that we left the Shunat Camp and went to Amman on our own. We lived in schools and mosques for two months, and then the Jordanian government brought us to Baqa'a. Again, we lived for two years in tents. Then the German Federal Labor League built prefab rooms, 4x3-1/2 meters, for each family. Whether the family had two persons or thirteen persons didn't matter. All the houses were the same size. We've been here ever since.

"My children are highly motivated. What is there to do but learn? The Palestinian depends on learning only. UNRWA provides elementary education until the Jordanian government takes over in secondary school. It is up to my children to learn. I have six boys and three girls— my youngest is fifteen. One of my children was from the first group of students to graduate from the University of Jordan. One boy has his master's degree in library studies. He earns 200 dinars a month. Two of them have degrees in English literature, one a master's in physical education, one in English, one in religion, one a master's in physics, and one is in preparatory class. All my children earned scholarships. They studied here, in Kuwait, and in Egypt at Yarmouk and Alexandria Universities. Some had two years of vocational community college. Each has his own house in Baqa'a now. I am in very high spirits. I will go back to my country with my children. Nothing will make me forget one leaf from one tree in our village."

She patted her son's hand. He returned her fond touch with a look of such gratitude and kindness that Leila and I smiled at each other in happiness.

Muhammad offered us more tea and then, after hesitating a moment, said, "I have decided to tell you this. My father and mother couldn't read or write. They guided us directly to be taught. They felt the Jews were stronger because they were educated. Their attitude affected our feeling about education. The way to go back home is to be educated. We haven't the military force to use against the enemy. We choose this way. If we're educated, we'll have strength to use against Israel to restore our rights. All of us know we'll go home. It's our responsibility to learn and to work toward that day.

"All these things are very far away for you in America. Now you may understand why we are angry with America. You support our enemy who kills us, who steals our land from us. If an enemy were one day to come to your house with tanks and guns and tell you they will take your house, your belongings, your land, and then they kill all but you and send you to a camp where you have nothing, what would you do? How would you live? Yes, these things are very far away for you. That's why no one understands our problem. Be glad you have your country."

His voice was low, but impassioned. There was no doubt in his mind that he and his people would emerge victorious from their sufferings.

After our visit to the busy social center, we bade respectful good-byes. On the way back to Amman, I asked Leila why the children still lived in the camp if all were educated and working. Her answer was very simple.

"They must serve as examples to their people."

CHAPTER ELEVEN

Who Will Help?

Our departure from Amman was scheduled for the first of July 1984, and many of the items needed to fill orders I had obtained on trips home were in the finishing stages. Leila and I had discussed several times the problems of obtaining the right material and quality finishing. Today we were to review all the needlework she had assigned to various women, some of which I had already picked up.

I'd left the door of our apartment open to coax a breeze through. Leila walked in jauntily, raring to go, asking, as always, "What is your news?" She was eager to review the orders so we could go to the camps early in the day.

"I want to bring you up to date on the situation with the woman supervising the completion of my needlework, Leila. I visited her early yesterday morning. She says when this order is finished, her women will not work on the cloth again. I am too fussy. I took ninety-eight pieces and left as many for her to correct. Please, Leila, in the future we must give the work to the women in Souf and use your tailor for finishing. Just look at these. Am I too fussy?"

Leila examined a few pieces, tossed them aside, and said, "You mustn't take them. You must tell Umm Y that you are sorry but the quality is not good, the finishing is not good. She must learn not to take bad work from her women. How will they learn to do good work if she accepts rubbish?"

"My sentiments exactly. I'm not screaming only because she's so generous to your projects. If I make her angry at me, I may make her angry at you."

"You're right. You mustn't shout. She's been very kind, just as Vivian said she would be when she asked me to begin working with Umm Y. That's what is important.

"Here is what we'll do. You will take all she has ready, even if they're not perfect. When my tailor finishes what I've given her, I'll exchange good pieces for those that are not so good. Visitors who buy small gifts here are not as demanding as merchants. We'll sell the ones you don't take, don't worry."

I felt much better. We descended the stairs to the street, got in the car, and started out on our day's activities, the first of which was to find a truck. Of course, I wanted to know why such a search was on our agenda.

"Here is the problem. We build the center, yes? We want the garbage hauled away, yes? What happens? The truck of the municipality outside Baqa'a doesn't come for four days. The garbage is piling up at all the pickup points in the camp. The people called me to say no one had come. It is hot. And because it's Ramadan they are fasting all day, and the smell of garbage is making them sick. They can't sit inside their houses all day in this heat. So I called the mayor to ask him why the truck didn't come. He told me it was broken, and that he has no other truck to send. I explained about the garbage. He said he knows, but what can he do until the only truck they have is fixed?"

"Can't another municipality be called to bring their trucks to the camp?"

"No. Only that one is authorized by UNRWA to pick up. So what can I do? Abu Zaki and I went to the mayor's house yesterday and took him to the dumps to see for himself. He said he was ashamed and sorry his truck was not running. He promised that beginning tomorrow if anything happens to the truck, he'll rent one and send it. He assured me it would not be repeated." She shook her head and sighed audibly.

"So," I said, "are we going to rent a truck for him?"

"No. I've found a donor. If I can find the right kind of truck here in Amman, the donor will buy it as his offering to the poor during Ramadan. We must take him a picture of the truck and tell him the cost. He will buy it within a week. Then do you know what I am thinking to do?" She turned to look at me, her eyes twinkling. It was disconcerting, as I have said, to ride with Leila. I had made peace with myself by keeping my eyes fastened on her while she drove. I felt that when she had my undivided attention it slowed her down. I wasn't able to take in much scenery, but then hurtling down the roads at full speed, horn blasting, had never relaxed me enough to enjoy it anyway.

"With you, my dear, there is no telling. I wouldn't attempt to keep up with your agile mind." She looked ahead at the traffic, satisfied with my answer.

"When the roof of the garbage center is secure, we will use it to lock up the truck. The donor will buy big metal containers that we will place all around the camp. The truck will pick up the containers, haul the garbage away, and bring the containers back. Instead of spending more money for sanitary centers, we will use the present one as a garage and we'll grade and pave the areas where the dumps were so the children will have a place to play and the women will have a place to sit."

"That is absolutely brilliant! How much will one truck and some containers cost?"

"I don't know—25,000 dinars or so with ten containers."

"And how much would the first center have cost? If you had paid for it, I mean."

"Eight thousand. So for the price of three centers, I take care of the entire camp."

"Leila, if you were in private industry in America, they would call you a genius. You'd be worth a fortune just for your ideas. Making them work besides would mean bonuses."

"I know." Her laughter rippled. "There is nobody like me."

"Did Abu Zaki know how smart you were when he married you?"

"I don't know if he thought I was smart, but he was convinced I would help the people. He gave me my start and encouraged me to see for myself. If he was a different kind of husband, I could never go out alone."

We pulled up in front of a small, unpretentious shop where a man was sitting at a desk behind the plate glass window. Leila parked on the sidewalk, as usual, and tooted the horn to beckon him outside. He came running to warn her away. That admonition ignored, he let her state her business. She had come to the right place. We walked into the cramped, dusty office. On the floor near the desk sat a large motor for inspection by prospective buyers. There was no showroom, no small office in which sales pressure could be applied, no lovely new vehicles to inspect, no used vehicles for that matter. Only one battered desk and the chair and the motor. An open staircase, with no railings, led to the second floor. All Leila had to say to the slightly bored, slightly patronizing clerk was that she wished to buy a truck. When he recovered, he rushed us up the steps to the manager's office, less cramped but just as dusty. In no time, she had the pictures and prices of a Mercedes loader and the metal containers, and we were on our way to her tailor, Umm Imad.

The seamstresses were chattering excitedly when Umm Imad opened her door. The mother of a bride had just delivered a magazine picture from which her daughter's dress was to be copied, along with the beaded fabric and the netting for the veil and train. They showed us the picture. The design was elaborate and richly detailed—a dress any bride would be thrilled to have. Only her measurements were given to Umm Imad. The charge for cutting, sewing, and fitting without a pattern was, in American money, 150 dollars.

A thin, wan little woman sat in a corner of the living room, wearing the long coat and scarf required by her religion. In her arms lay a small girl, all eyes, wearing a western-style pinafore and blouse. The fragile child showed no curiosity and made no sound.

After Umm Imad inspected the pieces I had brought with me, she assured Leila she would complete my order and replace the pieces I couldn't accept. She and Leila had a short conversation in Arabic with many smiles and *aywas*, meaning "yes," and we prepared to leave.

"We are taking Umm Ghassan to Marka Camp," said Leila. "It is a very long way from here. They will not let her take the chair on the bus, and the taxi is too expensive, so we are giving her a ride."

Umm Ghassan was the wan lady. She rose from an old metal chair with a vinyl seat and back rest and almost reverently dusted it off, holding her child in her arms all the while. When she tried to pick up the chair, I took it from her and carried it down to the car. By the time we all got in, Leila had visited a grocer and had bought a large bag of pasta.

Umm Ghassan and Leila spoke little. As we passed a bakery, Leila suddenly backed up around a corner and jammed on the brakes. My heart flew to my mouth. I got out and brought the owner back to the car, and she gave him an order for baked goods and sent me back in to fetch it. I staggered back to the car with kilos and kilos of bread and toast.

I learned that Umm Ghassan's little girl, whose name was Palestine, was four years old, and that she was dying from tuberculosis and other diseases in her lungs. The students at the medical center received good lessons from her strange condition and had operated on her many times. I asked Leila how she had met Umm Ghassan.

"Her husband was very, very ill. She has four children. When I met her four years ago, in 1980, they were six, five, four years, and the baby three months. All their relatives are in the West Bank. Because they had no money, some people donated a garage to them. When I was told about them, I went to see for myself. It was winter, and the room was cold because of the spaces in the walls. The little garage was on the side of a hill, and water seeped in. The four children were lying on a thin mattress on the floor. There were no windows and no doorway. Everyone who wished to enter had to raise the big garage door. Her thirty-two-year-old husband, so thin and ill, was lying in a corner of the room. Umm Ghassan was thirty-five and complained about a backache. How could I solve her many problems?"

Leila turned back to look at me with her question. I gripped the edge of the seat, saying, "How, Leila, how?" loudly, while muttering under my breath, "Please look at the road."

"There was no family in Amman, no relatives, nobody. Who would be responsible for this family? Some friends and I went to UNRWA and asked for a piece of land in the camp to build a room for her. UNRWA donated the land, my people donated materials, and the people in the camp built the house without taking one penny. The only land available at Marka was next to the sewage. Meanwhile, we took her husband to the military hospital and met with the doctors. They sent a social worker to study the family's situation and then operated to change two blood vessels in his heart at no cost. Had he paid, the charge would have been 2,000 dinars.

"After the family was settled in the house, Umm Ghassan said that little Palestine had been sick all her four years. At the hospital, the doctors diagnosed lung and liver disease and made incisions in her chest to drain the pus. Umm Ghassan could not afford the nutritious diet the doctors recommended. Every six months Umm Ghassan gives blood to her child. Her other children are often ill because of the garbage and open sewers.

Umm Ghassan is the sole support of the family, and the money she earns must be used for food. There is nothing extra for medicine. I sent her to Umm Imad, who cuts dress pieces and gives them to her to finish. She works while the children sleep. She earns thirty to forty dinars a month using the sewing machine I gave her."

We turned into the entrance of Marka Camp. It was more depressing than Baqa'a. The ruts and potholes were bigger, the pathways narrower, the people more listless as they moved to avoid the car. We bounced and bumped over two kilometers and parked on a steep hill overlooking Umm Ghassan's house. She carried her daughter into the house and came back to help me climb down the incline. Leila, nimble-footed, had no problem navigating her way to the house.

On a small plot of earth overhanging the sewage ditch there was a tiny vegetable garden. Around the house there were olive trees, which provided olives, oil, and shade, but I didn't see any flowers. There was no space. A water tank rested on top of the house, which was level with the pathway. We took off our shoes and went inside.

In the sitting room were two pieces of furniture, one a dilapidated table covered with a sheet, on which sat the sewing machine, and the other the empty box of a television set, used as a table for a miniature black-and-white TV. Partway up the wall was a narrow cement ledge, designed to be a cupboard base. On the ledge were eleven plastic flowerpots, a present from a man who owned a pot factory. When families helped Umm Ghassan, she gave them a pot with cuttings from her little garden. The archway between the sitting room and sleeping room was unfinished, exposing raw cement. Two curtained windows ventilated the entire house; they were near the ceiling to conserve wall space for leaning when sitting on the floor. A large, cheap weaving hung on the sitting room wall. The residents of this Muslim house thought it portrayed a family, and it did: Mary and Joseph were praying over Jesus. A small black-and-white photo of Neil Diamond had been cut from a magazine and was pasted to the wall. Perhaps he resembled a family member.

The kitchen, three steps up from the sleeping room, contained an Arab-style gas stove for baking the daily bread, a two-burner hot plate, a few pans and dishes on the two shelves above the cement ledge, which was to have been the kitchen cupboard base, and an old, small refrigerator, which contained only a plastic bowl of frozen water. A large bag of rice and a tin of flour sat on the floor. A fluorescent light and a small narrow window provided minimal light.

In the sleeping room were two metal wardrobes, one with bedding, the other with neatly stacked family clothing. The pit latrine was outside. It flowed out from a hole to the drainage ditch directly below them. Flies and mosquitoes from the ditch had bitten the children's arms and legs into permanent black welts.

When I put down the chair, two little girls immediately rushed in and sat on it. Then each one tried it again and again, for just an instant. It provided entertainment for a long time; it was the first chair the family had owned. Umm Ghassan pulled out a mattress and motioned for us to sit. She began to boil water to make us some tea, and though I wanted to decline, it is sometimes more important to save a person's pride than their food. As she made the tea, she told us her story.

CHAPTER TWELVE

If You Learn to Count One, Two, You Will Reach a Million

"We are originally from Dayr Aban, a village in the Jerusalem District of Palestine. When the soldiers came in 1948, we hid in the caves and came back at night to our village to get food. The Israeli soldiers shouted at us, saying, 'If you come back again, we will kill you.' We had no food or water. When we thought the Israelis had gone and that no one was left in the village, we came back. The soldiers put my father against the wall of the mosque and shot him before our eyes. My husband's father was also killed. My husband was only nine months old.

"My aunt shouted for them to stop. She jumped on the back of a soldier to make him put his gun down. They pulled her off, threw her to the ground, and shot her. Ten bullets. She was jerking with the impact of the bullets. 'Next time you return,' they said, 'you will be killed like this chicken.' My aunt was sixteen years old."

As she said this, Leila softly interpreting, tears rolled down her cheeks. Leila took her hand and held it for the rest of the story.

"We were three girls and three boys. My mother took us and fled to Amman. I was the youngest, carrying my bottle as we ran. It took us fifteen days to reach Amman, a one-day drive. Thousands of people were following us. Some people died from the bombs, some from shooting by the soldiers. My mother started working in houses here so she could help us children. The oldest was only ten years.

"There were 500 people in our village. Each family had its own land. Wells were beside our land. We could plant our food, eat, or sell it; we had clean water, fresh air, and a big area. We had chickens and bought goat's milk from the shepherds. Some people owned goats so they sold cheese, yogurt, and milk. Others, like us, cared for the land. We made our bread in an outside oven. There was room for cooking. Life was smooth, not like this.

"We still have family living in Deir Aban, on fifteen dunums. They plant and sell in Jerusalem and Bethlehem to survive. They have electricity and sewage systems, and everything is clean. My cousin is married to my sister. The Israelis came and took three-fourths of our land. Some of the owners died, and then the Israelis took my father's share. Now they will not give us a bridge pass to return to our land. My mother used to make our dresses by hand. Now we can't buy thread or material, we have no money, so the traditions from our village cannot be sewn into the material.

"My husband and I married here in 1974. He's a driver. We went to Germany in 1976 to find work, and he became a chauffeur. One day he collapsed on his job, so the German government returned him to Amman. We arrived here with him unable to work, with no house and no money. We had two boys and two girls. It was a very hard time.

"When my husband got sick, they discovered he had a heart defect from birth. He can't work. He has no car. Sometimes my child spends twenty or thirty days in the hospital. I must travel to see her. It costs money if I ride the bus to the hospital from Marka. I must wait one to two hours sometimes, carrying my child while I wait.

"Without the work from Umm Imad, I'd have to beg. It would be the only way I could survive. Even though I have relatives there, I'm not allowed to go back to the West Bank. I took this chair from Umm Imad because until now I do most of the work on the floor, and it is bad for my backache. Just now my husband's brother and his five girls and their boy are with us. The brother isn't well. He needs an operation. He can't find work that won't cause him bad pain. He has no money for an operation, no money to pay their rent. The owner is looking for him. If he can't pay the three months' rent he owes, he will be put in jail. He's hiding in my house with his family.

"My mother has high blood pressure, diabetes, and chronic asthma. She lives with her brother except when he can't find work. Then she stays with me. We have meat twice a month, otherwise, potatoes, tomatoes, and soup. We cut the bread up into the soup and eat it. Today, because of your food gifts, we'll have tea and toast at three and macaroni tonight."

She paused to ask if we would like more tea. When we politely refused, she continued.

"Once a week I go to Umm Imad's to learn the finishing and more about sewing. I bring home ten pieces. In this way I can learn to do more work. I can speak German and used to make cakes and puddings to sell, but the government stopped me because of the diseases. Now Umm Zaki has told me to keep a sample of a cut from her daughters' dresses, so I can sew for her family.

"I'd like it if medical treatment could be available at Marka Hospital nearby, so I wouldn't have to take my children so far, and my husband could get better attention. Even the dentist comes only twice a week, and that's to remove teeth. If we want them fixed, we must go to Amman or Zarqa. It costs three dinars to come and go. We can't pay, so most children lose their teeth. There is no doctor at night. If the children have fevers, or if it's winter and it snows for two or three days, the doctors won't come, and the little ones become seriously ill.

"My children have nothing but their certificates for good grades. All of them work very hard. That's how they will get out of this place. I must keep them going to the hospitals so that they can remain well enough to get an education. Their job at home is to collect tin cans so I can plant herbs in them. I transfer them to pots when they grow big enough for presents to people who help me.

"I live so far from the camp's hot food center that I can't carry the children there. There is no transportation inside the camp. If I don't feed the children at the center, I cannot have the food. Every month I receive one dinar's worth of flour from UNRWA. They give me only medicine, like aspirin and penicillin, so I must travel to Jordan University Hospital to obtain care and medicine for my daughter. My husband is often too weak to travel. He can't walk from here to the bus.

"My neighbors are in worse shape than I am. I pay no rent because Umm Zaki built my house. It has a ceiling instead of the tin roof. It has three rooms instead of two. If I become sicker in the future, we can live in two rooms and rent out this room for fifteen dinars a month."

I asked Umm Ghassan to tell me when she had been the happiest, of her good memories after she left her village.

Her pale face lit up. "The day I met Umm Zaki."

We said good-bye, realizing we were her only company from outside her family, her only hope for her tenuous future. The courage and perseverance of this tiny, tired woman was heart-wrenching. She was imprisoned in a routine that would be broken only when her children, if they lived, obtained the educational qualifications that would change their lives and hers.

Leila drove through the deep potholes and the large rocks protruding between the tire tracks. As we bumped along I gripped the dashboard to keep from hitting the roof.

"Leila, how do you keep going? There are so many problems. They are all so tragic and so unsolvable. How do you do it?"

"If you want to do anything, you have to start with one step. If you learn to count one, two, you will reach 1 million. I see the difference. I follow the ones I help and the ones I don't help. In the future, five or six years from now, I will see what happens to her if I help her and if I don't help her. That is why I made the clubs at Souf, Baqa'a, and Hussein camps. The children must have a place to go after school. Instead of stealing and quarreling, they go to the clubs. With education, they'll learn to serve the people instead of stealing from them. You have both good and bad everywhere. If I help a hundred children now, there will be a hundred families later who'll be educated and well brought up and who will help others because they were helped. In the long run, there will be thousands.

"I owe my ability to help to my husband. We always cared for the future and saved our money for the black days. I never rented a car or spent my time buying clothes. We never spent money on foolish things. When we bought land, it was cheap. When my children needed money for school, we sold the land. After all, Abu Zaki spent most of his life working in government. He's not a merchant. But he gave me the time, the money, and the car to be sure I helped poor people. He said I should make something useful for myself instead of visiting and so on."

It was two o'clock, time for Leila to return home to feed her family, part of her "tax" for doing the work. Even though the children are grown, they are under her roof, and therefore must be cared for as fully as if they were still in school.

Leila sees to it that the house glows with cleanliness and does the first food preparation before leaving in the morning. She doesn't use instant food or many canned foods. The fresh produce in Amman is so flavorful and attractive, ours in the States tastes like cardboard in comparison.

Leila's efficiency is remarkable. The telephone is next to the refrigerator and food preparation area. It rings constantly. She talks, cuts, and chops, and obtains new items from the refrigerator without missing a stroke of the knife. She sets the table from dishes kept on open drying racks nearby, continues talking on the phone, places the serving dishes on the table, kicks the refrigerator door shut with her foot, and washes her utensils. When the conversation is over, lunch is ready, and the kitchen is again spotless.

After serving, she washes the dishes, takes her shower, changes into another long embroidered dress, and announces that we are ready to leave for Baqa'a. It is three o'clock.

"The most important thing is to put something in their mouths," she said, as we took the elevator to the first floor. "There is an Arabic saying: 'Rely always on the woman. Whatever she does, if she does not cook, she is not a good wife and mother.' I shop, I clean, I iron, I cook, I get all the things the family needs. The children are tended, my husband is tended. They are happy. When they are happy, my mind is free to do my mission."

Palestine died a few months after our visit.

1998 – Umm Ghassan – Her husband died of a heart attack in 1990. Her daughters married. Her sons became carpentry apprentices and continue living with their mother.

CHAPTER THIRTEEN

Home Again—1985

I WENT TO THE MIDDLE EAST KNOWING MUCH
more about Israel than I did about the thousands of years of history of
Palestine and the Middle East. Having decided to become better informed
about the area and the conflict between the Arabs and the Israelis, I told
Leila I would visit our local library immediately upon our return to the
States and begin immersing myself in the issues that so affected her
people. Leila trained her usual patient gaze on me and said quietly, "There
will be no books in your library, Pat."

We lived in a major city then. Naively, I assured her that our library
contained thousands, maybe tens of thousands of volumes, that it would
provide answers to all my questions, and that I would write often of my
progress.

There wasn't much to write. Of the many, many shelves of books on
the heroes and heroines of Israel, its brief history and politics, the history
and politics of the Middle East, there was only one slight volume written
from an Arab point of view. It was presented by people as far removed
from the Arab-Israeli conflict as I was: a debate between an American Jew
and an Egyptian on the "Question of Palestine."

Difficult as it was and still is to obtain titles that provide either objective analyses or the Arab side of the story, I continued to read, read, and read. When I came across Henry Cattan's book, *Palestine, the Arabs and Israel,* written in 1969, I learned that the Palestinian Arabs are a pre-Islamic people who already lived in Palestine as well as other parts of the Middle East before Islam. The Palestinians of today descend from the Canaanites and other early tribes and "have lived continuously and without interruption in their country since the dawn of history. Their settlement in Palestine can be traced back to at least forty centuries. There were infusions of other racial elements into the Palestinian stock, mainly from the Greeks, the Romans, the Muslim Arabs and the Crusaders. But this Palestinian stock, which comprises both Muslims and Christians, continued to constitute the main element of the population until the majority of the original inhabitants were displaced by the Israelis in 1948."[1]

Besides the Muslim and Christian Arabs, small communities of Jews, Armenians, Assyrians, and Kurds lived among the Palestinians. "The Jews did not integrate into the ethnic stock formed by the original people of Palestine.... From the lst century of our era until the 20th century, the Jews had almost ceased to exist in Palestine.... Up to the 19th century the Jewish population of Palestine had increased very little.... [In 1800, they] numbered 8,000.... In 1880 their number did not exceed 20,000... [and] in 1918, 56,000, less than 10 percent of the total population.... After the end of the First World War and following the Balfour Declaration there was a wave of Zionist Jewish immigration into Palestine. The Palestine census in 1922 gave their number as 83,794 out of a total population of 757,182."[2]

Between 1518 and 1917, Palestine was an administrative unit of the Ottoman Empire, with all of its citizens enjoying equal civil rights. In 1887–88 it was divided into the three administrative units of Acre,

Nablus, and Jerusalem, with Jerusalem and its environs given a special status that linked it directly to Constantinople (now Istanbul) rather than being dependent on the provincial governor.[3]

Then came World War I. Encouraged by British promises of independence, Hussein bin Ali of the Hejaz (Sharif of Mecca) joined the Allied armies, and Arabs from Syria, Lebanon, and Palestine answering his call for revolt, joined the ranks of the Allies and fought with them against the Turks. Their efforts, directed by the British officer T. E. Lawrence (known as Lawrence of Arabia), contributed substantially to the Allied victory.

Ruth Jordan, in her book *Daughter of the Waves: Memories of Growing up in Pre-War Palestine*, described the war years as "harsh ... with heavy taxation, compulsory labor on the roads and railroads, confiscation of property and widespread starvation." Furthermore, "Turkey and her allies used Palestine as a base for their assault on Egypt and the Suez Canal, and the inhabitants were required to provide supplies for the 4th Turkish Corps."[4]

Conscription was also introduced, and the inhabitants, regardless of religion, were forced to serve in the army of a corrupt regime that many of them despised. Fuel for the Hejaz Railway was obtained from the already nearly depleted forests and even from the olive trees, upon which the rural population was so dependent.

In 1917, General Allenby led the British into Palestine and ended 400 years of Ottoman domination. While the politicians debated the future of the region, "a British military command was set up under the title of Occupied Enemy Territory Administration (South). The League of Nations later entrusted Great Britain with a mandate to govern the occupied territories on both sides of the river Jordan, and a former cabinet minister, the Jewish Sir Herbert Samuel, was appointed first High Commissioner for Palestine. On June 30, 1920, Major General Bols, the British military governor in charge of OETA (South), relinquished his command with a simple chit of paper: 'Handed over to Sir Herbert Samuel, one Palestine, complete.'"[5]

It is well established that despite their contribution to the Allied victory, the Palestinian Arabs were betrayed and their homeland given away by the West to a foreign minority. "In a letter of July 14, 1915, Sherif Hussein of the Hejaz, obviously looking for postwar gains, asked that Britain recognize the independence of all Arab countries south of Turkey with the exception of Aden. He did not mention Egypt.... [On October 24], 1915, Sir Henry McMahon, High Commissioner for Egypt and the Sudan ... [replied] that he was authorized by the British Government to pledge that Britain was prepared to 'recognize and uphold the independence of the Arabs' in all the regions lying within the frontiers proposed by the Sherif."[6]

Meanwhile, Britain had secretly concluded an agreement with France to divide the Middle East into spheres of influence that ignored the commitments made to Hussein. Another collusive agreement in 1920 decided that the French would control the regions now known as Syria and Lebanon, and the British would control what is now known as Jordan, Iraq, and Israel with its occupied territories. Hussein learned of his betrayal when Russia's new Bolshevik government discovered the secret agreement in the Tsarist archives and published it. In the ensuing brouhaha, Britain and France issued a joint statement assuring the Arabs they would be liberated from their oppressive rule and promising they would set up "national governments and administrations that would derive their authority from free exercise of initiative and choice by the indigenous populations."[7]

In November 1918, Emir Faisal, the Sharif's son, went abroad for the first time to London and Paris, but could not, in spite of T. E. Lawrence's pleas on his behalf, persuade the Allies to fulfill the promises made to his father.

The McMahon pledges were undermined further by Arthur Balfour, the British Foreign Secretary, even before Faisal reached London. The Balfour Declaration, which the League of Nations incorporated into the Mandate, was issued November 2, 1917. The text of the Declaration, which has remained a bitter bone of contention ever since, stated that:

> His Majesty's Government view with favour the establishment in Palestine of a national home for the Jewish people, and will use their best endeavours to facilitate the achievement of this object, it being clearly understood that nothing shall be done which may prejudice the civil and religious rights of existing non-Jewish communities in Palestine, or the rights and political status enjoyed by Jews in any other country.

This document, the result of intensive lobbying by Chaim Weizmann, who was to become the first President of Israel, laid the foundation for all subsequent Zionist development.[8]

In addition to reading, I joined Middle East peace groups in order to obtain literature about our government's activities and policies in the area, and most importantly, I began to question what I heard on television and read in the newspaper. Over time, I am beginning to become more informed, which has led to my ability to recognize, belated though it may be, more subtle forms of discrimination.

Hoping to promote an atmosphere of curiosity and conciliation through the arts, I obtained through the good efforts of an Arab friend in Jordan enough fine examples of traditional needlework from each village to round out my collection and to launch a museum-quality exhibit in a public space. While initial responses are always enthusiastic, I have been unsuccessful to date in obtaining space for a showing. The most incredible excuse I have received thus far is that the work is "too confrontive" to be put on public display. An opportunity to educate people about another culture through splendid examples of folk art—folk art that may die with this generation—is in danger of being lost because the keepers of such spaces feel it may be politically offensive to a potential viewer, or more ingratiatingly, to a potential donor.

When I speak before groups interested in my experiences with the refugees, I begin by showing them pieces of the needlework and telling some of the stories of the proud and talented women who created them. I explain that I would like to offer them some information about the Arab-Israeli conflict that they might not have read or heard, information that might help them make an informed decision in supporting our government's budget and military policies. Then I tell them that the struggle between Israel and the Palestinians has continued for more than sixty years, and that a population of nearly 4 million has lived for most of that time under military occupation while an entirely new generation has grown up without civil rights and suffering the humiliations, impotence, frustrations, and sense of helplessness that are concomitant with such a situation. Many Israelis now recognize the dilemma posed by demographic reality: more Arabs than Jews in the entire area. Should Israel annex the occupied territories and grant citizenship to all the residents, it would cease to be a Jewish state. If, on the other hand, it chooses to annex without granting citizenship, Israel would find itself in the position of instituting an unequal society—an unhappy choice for a country that perceives itself as being just and democratic. Thus, the maintenance of the status quo because of the inability or unwillingness to make such a hard choice.

Through a variety of mechanisms, Israel has taken over about 52 percent of West Bank land and some 40 percent of Gaza. The settlers who have been allowed to settle illegally in these areas are a continuous provocation to the Palestinians. Since Israeli civil law does not apply to the territories, the military uses extraordinary measures to protect the settlers and suppress Arab dissent.

Concern for the rights and welfare of the Palestinians must go beyond seeking a more humane regime of occupation. Resolution will come only with a just settlement of the conflicting claims, guarantees of security and recognition of the right of self-determination for everyone.

Until there is reconciliation among these people, the mothers of today's politicized generation can do little more than continue to stir the souls of their children through their embroidery, with the hope that the next generation will experience the rich and diverse culture exemplified in the weavings as a free and independent people.

PHOTOS

Leila at age 2 with her mother and father

Leila examines needlework in progress

Volunteers help to create a street,
later named Umm Zaki Street, in Baqa'a Camp

Volunteers build sewage channels

Leila with school officials and students
on opening day of the library/social center

Volunteer helps to rebuild a house for a family of seven whose father died

Home economics department of girls' high school

Graduation day at boys' secondary school

Leila instructs volunteers on a construction project

A young girl helps to build another street

Two very young helpers take time out for a photo

Leila and volunteers admire prepared sanitation center site

November 2010

Leila and I admire murals in the school yard
of Baqa'a elementary school

Students encircle us

Leila and school principal Raeda abou alrob

Leila and I stand on school steps with girls and alrob

Third grader sings "Who Will Ring the Bell" in English

Classmates accompany the singer

Students raise a balloon to request permission to speak

Leila reminds students to be proud of their school and themselves

A student asks Leila a question

Leila and I with principal alrob and camp official in preschool playroom created with donations obtained by Leila

Children play in the preschool

I'm in the well-furnished, well-lighted library with shelves and shelves of books

We stand together before a mural
showing women in a traditional Palestinian village

EPILOGUE

Twenty-five years have passed. Preparing to return to Jordan on a two-year contract beginning in January 1985, we sold our house and put our belongings in storage. When my husband suggested we spend the holidays in South Texas with his mother, who would otherwise be all alone, I agreed. The holidays came and went. We didn't. After many months of clinging to the hope that we'd soon be winging our way to the Middle East, I concluded it wasn't to be. Instead of becoming more immersed in the Arab culture, I found myself struggling to understand Texan. Part of adjusting to small town living, where the local Dairy Queen served free coffee on Mondays in a cup with your name on it, was finding new ways to structure our lives. Lee became a prize-winning sculptor, represented in fine art galleries. I became a fine craft artist. We entered a new chapter in our relationship and new careers. Each time we arranged to travel to the Middle East, we were forced to cancel because of unrest in the area.

In March of 2010, I lost my beloved husband and soul mate. In July, I was in a serious auto accident. The doctors told me I was lucky to be alive, and that I'd better make all my dreams come true. One of those dreams was seeing Leila and Yahya once again. My family took a trip to Egypt in November to help all of us heal, with an extension to Jordan for me.

I was picked up at the Amman airport by Dema, a relative of the Phoenix travel agent who'd made all the arrangements. As we drove, she told me that until she called Leila to get directions to her house, she didn't know she would be delivering me to a relative, one she hadn't seen in years. By this time, nothing surprised me, except what I was seeing from the car windows.

The city I knew so well and had walked about so easily was gone. Empty fields where I'd watched Bedouin women milking their sheep were now filled with hotels, boutiques, restaurants, and shops of every kind and description. Traffic clogged the streets. Drivers thought nothing of passing on the right, even when the farthest lane was occupied. Traveling by car required nerves of steel and a healthy heart, as each outing was like an Olympic event.

The population in Jordan has increased by hundreds of thousands of people displaced by the wars in Iraq, Lebanon, and Kuwait. Half a million Iraqis brought with them ambition and a desire to replace the businesses they'd lost. There are now a hundred Iraqi restaurants. Amman is becoming the medical capital of the Middle East. Doctors from all over the world are practicing there, and thousands of students are enrolled in various fields of medicine.

We climbed and climbed until we were in Abdoun, high over the city, in a quiet residential neighborhood. We pulled up in front of one of the many wrought iron gates that protect the properties. Dema got out of the car and rang the bell. I saw an outline of the woman coming toward her glass entry, called out "No this isn't it," and beckoned Dema to return to the car.

"You haven't seen her for a long time. Are you sure?" she asked. I was, and edgy with excitement and impatience. We passed a few more gates and she stopped again and rang the bell. Again I saw a woman's outline coming toward the glass door. I leaped out of the car as the gate opened and ran up the steps. "Leila, it's me, it's me. I'm so happy to see you!" She held out her arms and we embraced for a long moment. I was back, back with my wise, compassionate friends.

Leila's house is a sanctuary in the midst of Amman's feverish construction. She ushered us through the glassed-in sun porch into a cool, high-ceiling living room, tastefully decorated with contemporary furniture and bright with sunlight. We followed her and the enticing aromas of spices and roasting chicken to the adjoining dining area to the luncheon prepared in our honor. Their healthy Mediterranean diet of many vegetables, chicken or lamb, and fruit is one we could benefit from. Dema was working and left after lunch. I wanted nothing more than to hear everything that had happened during the many years we'd lost our connection.

Leila's face was changed. In 1989, five years after my departure, she'd had a stroke that paralyzed the left side of her face. Two operations corrected much of the palsy, but traces remain. She was on the operating table for eight hours to lift her skin and now has acupuncture sessions. Allergic to antibiotics, recovery was long and difficult.

She has high blood pressure, asthma, and diabetes, and has had gallstones removed. Despite her health issues, she radiated her usual purposefulness and efficient competence. Thirteen months before my visit she'd fallen in her living room. No one heard her calls for help for quite some time. It was feared she wouldn't walk again. She prayed that if she recovered she would devote herself to the elementary schools in Baqa'a Camp. After three months of daily physical therapy she was ready to resume her life and keep her promise.

From the teachers Leila contacted, she obtained the names of the poor, poorer and poorest children at one of the most rundown schools in the Camp, with 2,200 students ages six to thirteen years. Baqa'a Elementary had been built fifteen years before with a donation from Japan. The school was in shambles with no heat, broken windows, and dilapidated desks and chairs. The children sat on the floors, many without sufficient clothing to keep out the cold. Since UNRWA had no funds for books for the children, Leila's friends donated 500 of them. Dr. Walid Sheree donated jackets and underwear to the poorest children. Others donated 2,000 dinars to make a high fence to protect the children and prevent outsiders from entering the school. As we talked, it was decided that I should see for myself the changes that devotion and donations had made in so many young people's lives.

Later in the evening we shared news about our own children and grandchildren, and I surprised her with the announcement that I now had three great-grandchildren. Hearing about the closeness of her family and how all of them support each other in good times and bad, I reflected on the differences between Leila's culture and mine. We chase employment, wherever it might be, leaving friends and family behind and perhaps returning for holidays or not. Family closeness is treasured. In the Middle East it is expected. We miss so much.

"Surviving the accident gave me a second chance, Leila. I gained an even greater appreciation of my family. If I didn't have them, I would move here, rent the apartment in your house, and just work with you." Leila reached from her recliner to mine and squeezed my hand. "It's like we've never been apart. We've picked up right where we left off."

"I know, Pat. Perhaps when people read your book they will see that we are just like them. We love our families, we visit our friends, and we help those less fortunate. Is it not the same?"

"It is. Exactly."

When it was time to say goodnight, she directed me to their vacant apartment on the floor below for showering and sleeping, a peaceful arrangement for all.

Early the next morning, after breakfasting on eggs, cheese and toast served in her spacious kitchen, she handed me a long, black, embroidered dress to put on over my clothes. She wore the same, adding a shawl for warmth. We started for Baqa'a Camp. I marveled that she would chance the drive. I'd brought along a bottle of water and was about to take a drink when Leila took it from me. She stopped the car next to a garbage truck and handed it to the worker. "It's hot," she said. "He needs it more than you." And of course he did.

As we navigated traffic, Leila explained that there are sixteen schools in Baqa'a Camp, eight of them serving elementary students. From grades 1 through 3 boys and girls attend together. From grades 4 through 10, they are separated. All are rundown. All need help. UNRWA was founded to help the Palestinian refugees until they return to their country. However, it wishes to end that responsibility in Jordan and has cut financial aid to both the refugees and the schools, so many private schools give donations directly. She reminded me that The American Community School of Amman has supported the Camp for over twenty-five years. They gave several of the schools their entire library of a thousand books in Arabic when it was renovated. The student council donates the proceeds of its fundraisers. Samar Abu Gazaleh, the current librarian, replaced Vivian Daher, the generous American friend who introduced me to Leila so many years ago. Vivian and her family now live in the U.S.

Our conversation was interrupted when Leila drove into the grassless school yard and parked near the entrance. Gone was the tiny social center with its cheap shelving and few books. Gone was the school I'd described as nothing more than an unlit room with benches, broken windows, and a table and chair for the teacher. In its place was a modern two-story building surrounded by a tall cement block wall. As we walked toward it through throngs of children, two teachers came out to greet us. They welcomed Leila to a microphone to talk with the children. In Arabic she thanked them for their care of their surroundings and encouraged them to continue showing pride in their school and in themselves. The children listened politely, and when she finished, they rushed forward to go to their classes, smiling shyly and reaching out to touch her as they passed by. We were guided into the principal's office where I was gratified to see that she had a real desk, a computer, a glass-fronted bookcase, two guest chairs, a sofa and four windows with gauzy curtains. Visiting her that day were Dr. Saber Dawoud Abdel Kareem Ali, head of all the Jordan Camps for UNRWA, Raeda Abu AlRub, head teacher, and Inas Al Shoubaki, assistant head teacher.

We began our tour of the building. The corridor walls were filled with colorful murals painted by talented local artist Tayel Muqbil, who had generously extended his work to the walls surrounding the school yard. The children are so pleased with the depictions of their culture that they don't deface them.

Classes are held in two shifts – 7:00 to 11:30 a.m. and 11:30 to 4 p.m. with thirty-five teachers, one director and one janitor per shift. Forty to forty-five students per class sit at desks built for two. There are blackboards. The children have books, pencils and paper. Each desk has a little plastic bag hanging from it for any litter that might accumulate. The windows are unbroken, the floors are clean, and there are fans and electric lights. Along with the teachers are teachers-in-training who assist them. The minuscule library/social center of so long ago has been replaced by a large inviting room with a full-time librarian, tables, chairs, study areas and shelving to hold the hundreds of books. UNRWA requires the children to wear uniforms. They are purchased for or donated to the 700 children unable to afford them. Leila and other donors provide jackets, boots and clothing so that the older children can play in the school yard.

It is cold in Amman in the winter. Leila has created an indoor playroom where the youngest children can go between shifts, with toys and equipment donated by generous benefactors. There are child-size chairs for circle games. The walls are brightly colored, with letters of the alphabet displayed as large paper cutouts. The children were too busy making puzzles, riding the seesaw, or coloring to pay any attention to us.

We said our goodbyes with happy hearts, grateful for the care given to the school by staff, students and Herima Dheb, the school's director for the last three years.

Back on the road, Leila and I discussed the condition of refugees everywhere who are separated from relatives, rituals, their stories and traditions. What happens to them when they graduate from high school, if they do? Leila certainly knew. She told me there are now 62,000 students in college on the West Bank supported by individual families. Many of their fathers have been in jail without charge for years. Others went to Iraq and didn't return. The fathers of several students, truck drivers who traveled regularly between Amman and Baghdad, were robbed and shot. The trucks carried fuel oil to Baghdad and returned with foodstuffs. The situation has made food very expensive. Formerly a kilo of tomatoes was 10 piasters. Now they cost one dinar per kilo (currently $1.40). Rent for one room is 150 dinars per month in the poorest areas, plus 30 more for electricity. Students can't afford it. Currently, Leila and Yahya support four students, two boys and two girls.

Before returning home, we made one last stop to see my long ago friend Miriam Abulaban, who'd also given me pillow covers to sell in the States with the understanding that I'd send her payments by check. This went well until a check wasn't cashed and my letters weren't returned. I explained to Leila that I'd brought money to pay for the remainder of the items if we could just find Miriam. I didn't want to be remembered as an ugly American who'd cheated an honest, hardworking woman. Her former business, done on her dining room table, is now a boutique selling dresses of many hues, decorated with the cross-stitched needlework that I'd so feared would disappear. The business is now in the hands of her daughters, but as luck would have it, Miriam was there. Gracious as always, saying her eyesight no longer allowed her to participate fully, she accepted my payment, telling customers who were being fitted that even after so many years her customers were always good to her. She gave me a lovely scarf as a memento of our visit, telling me it was perfect with my coloring. Who would know better?

On one of our outings I looked for the house with the penthouse apartment we'd rented, from which we could see the lights of Jerusalem. Formerly a grand mansion with an imposing façade, fruit orchard and complete apartment on each floor for sons and their brides whenever they would marry, today it is squeezed between a huge hotel and a boutique, the lone holdout on a commercial thoroughfare. Leila pointed out a building she'd rented years before to initiate a preschool. She supports the Jerusalem Society for Preschool Children, the Orphan Society and the Queen Alia Society for Deaf and Dumb Children, as well as helping families and students. To start the Jerusalem Society, which provides education and music classes for preschoolers, she rented a three-story building near Hussein Refugee Camp. Children with no parents or with one parent come to the facility and are picked up at the end of the day by older children or the parent. One hundred children receive day care. Donations go directly to the Society to hire teachers, pay rent, and to buy equipment and musical instruments for children three to six years of age. Samira Bitar, a friend from elementary school in

Jerusalem, has helped her since 1975 in this endeavor. Samira's son owns the Nestle water franchise in Amman and is very generous to the poor. The bridge from the donors to these societies is Leila. She's active in Save Our Souls, a European institution aiming to support orphans and widows, with offices in Jordan and Aqaba. Here, too, she is the bridge between the organization and the donors, collecting thousands of dollars in goods and services to be given directly to SOS by donors. She's assisted in her work by Dr. M. and N. Halabi, N. Barakat, I. Tahboub, S. Kleibo, R. Abulrub, I. Alsharif, and M. Labadi, all of whom use their own transportation to deliver donations. She talks to building owners, who then donate old items to Camp schools when they renovate.

In the evenings, after invited guests had departed, Leila and I sat side by side in recliners in her living room with our feet up, sipping hot, fragrant cups of tea. She told me more about her early life with Yahya, stories that put my years in Texas of living with my mother-in-law into perspective. For the first seven years of their marriage, they lived in Bethlehem in a three-bedroom apartment with Yahya's mother and three sisters. In 1952, his brother moved to Germany, one sister went to Egypt to study and another to Kuwait to teach. His mother and oldest sister remained. At that point they rented two apartments in Ramallah, with his mother and sister on one side and Leila's family on the other, with a door between for easy access. Each summer all his siblings returned to Ramallah for three months to stay with them.

After Yahya's deportation and auto accident, Leila took care of the children and struggled for years to get the signatures required by the Israeli government that would reunite them. Three years after the return of his identity card, they moved to Jordan permanently. After four years in Zarka, they again rented a house in Amman. By now Yahya's mother was sixty years old. His sister, now forty, worked at an orphanage for the next seven years. In 1980 they moved to another apartment in the doctors housing, where they were living when I met them.

Yahya and Leila saved pennies. They didn't go out in the evenings. They ate at home. Having lost everything again and again, material things had little meaning. They lived their philosophy. Their example of patience, tolerance and generosity wasn't lost on their children. To this day they donate clothing, reading materials and money to those less fortunate. Back then they donated their toys and clothing to the refugee children, asking Leila to choose them for the trip to a camp. "It's my turn, it's my turn," they would beg.

Today their children are successful parents of ten grandchildren, seven of whom are studying at university. Maysoon is married to a doctor, Monia is a teacher of teachers, son Zaki, a civil engineer, manages a large construction company specializing in apartment buildings, and son Amjad is studying for his doctorate at Harvard while working with a drug factory in Portugal.

Despite the passage of time, I learned that nothing has really changed. Not Leila's work, which continues one family, one charity, one school at a time. Not the fifteen schools awaiting Leila. Not Yahya's enthusiastic support. Not the poverty and misery in the camps.

As Mustafa said so eloquently twenty-five years ago, it is as if you'd put in a carbon.

APPENDIX A

"Leila Wahbeh—
Building Bridges Between
the Rich and the Poor"

Jordan Times **feature article, Tuesday, November 20, 2001**
by Jacky Sawalha

Outside Umm Zaki's home that overlooks the rolling wheat fields of Wadi Abdoun, a truck pulls up, the first of many, laden with eighty bags of donated dry foodstuffs and clothing to see 80 poor families through the month of Ramadan. After instructions are given, Nadia, the volunteer driver, sets off. Inside, the telephone rings, as it does at all hours of day and night, seven days a week. The caller gets straight to the point, "I wish to support 25 families on a daily basis during the month of Ramadan," as he/she knows that only the business at hand will be talked about. That 'business' is what has made Umm Zaki a household name in thousands of homes across the country for the last 40 years. These homes are the Palestinian refugee camps where they have been living for the 30–50 years since they were ousted from Palestine.

Umm Zaki, Leila Wahbeh, is a maverick philanthropist with a mesmerizing spirit of cheerful determination.

Born in Jerusalem in 1935 ... she was to meet her future husband, Yahya Wahbeh, a doctor of paediatrics who was the director of a government health centre in Bethlehem. ...Their wedding reception was the talk of the town; it was the first to be held in a hotel, which was a break from tradition and a challenge to the restrictive social norms that only allowed celebrations in the privacy of one's own home.

Leila was happy and fulfilled for the next ten years of her life, being mother to four children, pursuing her one hobby of embroidery and working with Yahya, who asked for her help to do something about the plight of widows and orphans.... Little did she know that one day she too would need assistance. One fateful night in 1967, the Israeli authorities came knocking on the door and took Yahya away at gunpoint. Leila would not see her husband again for two years. Filled with fear and despair she was galvanized into action and spent the next five years challenging the Israeli authorities to give her a reason for her husband's deportation to Jordan...along with seven other medical doctors.

Leila is a formidable opponent. She pursued her husband's case through the courts and eventually achieved her goal: an Israeli admission of no wrongdoing and the return of her husband's identity card. For the second time Leila picked up the pieces of her life and resettled with her husband in Amman, true to her conviction and that of her grandmother's, that "in order to achieve you must first survive."

...Leila's strength lies in her ability to create networks of charity; physically connecting those that have with those that have not. Money goes straight to those in need, as she believes that "God would provide if you open your eyes and invest in life not in bank accounts." She has no need for banks: "My life is a bank and the interest is the reward of giving." It was this philosophy that would be challenged time and time again, and she often found herself pursued in the courts by individuals who refused her ideals of giving assistance directly to those in need. But she always found encouragement when she needed it, as in Faiseh Abdel Majid, director of the Palestine School in Jabal Amman. "Push on, push on," she would tell her, "no one throws stones on a tree that grows apples." (This translates to "No one throws stones at rotten fruit.")

Leila is supported in her work by a small group of equally dedicated women who, like Samira Awad Bitar, an old classmate, and Nadia Barakat Hudhud, an excellent driver, would give unconditional help, such as acquiring an expensive, beautiful silk wedding dress, not wanted as it was ordered the wrong colour, and that is now rented for the cost of dry cleaning by young women who rent it for the day.

Another of her philosophies is to insist that donors accompany her on her rounds to see for themselves the deprivation and suffering of the poor. On a visit to an orphanage back in the 1980's....she asked ten-year-old Mohammad how he got a particularly nice looking hat. "I stole it" came the reply and it was then that she pursued his case to find out more. He was one of seven children whose mother was a widow and unable to care for her children due to ill health. With the help of her team, she made sure that Mohammad and his siblings went to school regularly: that his mother was provided with medical care, and that her bills for rent, water and electricity were paid until Mohammad graduated from school. He is now a successful lawyer, working in Abu Dhabi, who in turn helps Umm Zaki in her work. This is just one success story among hundreds, if not thousands, where lives have been turned around and dignity regained.

To these people, her people, she epitomizes all that is good in the world, for they have precious little else: she is there for them in the good times and the bad, she is their salvation and their hope and her home is always open to them. Hers is a network of charity that builds bridges of happiness on a daily basis between the rich and the poor. She continues to target the young on both sides of the social divide so that they grow up with a better understanding of life to help them build a better society in the future. She is indeed "a committee of one" as her friend, Pat Holt, American writer and journalist, would describe her.

APPENDIX B

What IS the United Nations Relief and Works Agency for Palestine Refugees in the Near East?

UNRWA provides assistance, protection, and advocacy for some 4.8 million registered Palestine refugees in the Middle East.

The Agency's services encompass education, health care, relief, camp infrastructure and improvement, community support, microfinance and emergency response, including in times of armed conflict.

Following the 1948 Arab-Israeli conflict, UNRWA was established by United Nations General Assembly resolution 302 (IV) of 8 December 1949 to carry out direct relief and works programs for Palestine refugees. The Agency began operations on 1 May 1950.

In the absence of a solution to the Palestine refugee problem, the General Assembly has repeatedly renewed UNRWA's mandate, most recently extending it until 30 June 2014.

Since its establishment, the Agency has delivered its services both in times of relative calm in the Middle East, and in times of hostilities.

UNRWA's work exemplifies an international commitment to the human development of Palestine refugees, helping them:

- acquire knowledge and skills
- lead long and healthy lives

- achieve decent standards of living
- enjoy human rights to the fullest possible extent.

UNRWA is unique in terms of its long-standing commitment to one group of refugees, and its contributions to the welfare and human development of four generations of Palestine refugees. Originally envisaged as a temporary organization, the Agency has gradually adjusted its programs to meet the changing needs of the refugees.

UNRWA provides education, health, relief, and social services to eligible refugees among the 4.8 million registered Palestine refugees in its five fields of operation:

- Jordan
- Lebanon
- Gaza Strip
- the Syrian Arab Republic
- the West Bank, including East Jerusalem

More than 1.4 million refugees, around one-third of the total, live in fifty-eight recognized camps, and UNRWA's services are located in or near these areas.

Unlike other United Nations organizations that work through local authorities or executing agencies, UNRWA provides its services directly to Palestine refugees. It plans and carries out its own activities and projects, and builds and administers facilities such as schools and clinics.

The Agency currently operates or sponsors over 900 installations with nearly 30,000 staff across the five fields. Because UNRWA services such as education and health care are the type of services normally provided within the public sector, the Agency cooperates closely with governmental authorities in the area of operations, which also provides some services to Palestine refugees.

See www.unrwa.org for detailed information.

APPENDIX C

UNRWA Statistics on Camps We
Visited—Jordan Field Office

Changes Between 1988 and 2011

		Baqa'a	Jebel el- Hussein	Suf	Marka
	Year Camp Erected	1968	1952	1967	1968
	Population & area				
	No. Dunams	1,400	367	500	917
	Initial Population	26,000	8,000	8,000	15,000
2011	*Population**	*110,031*	*28,939*	*18,214*	*48,087*
	Housing				
1988	Original Tent Shelters	5,000	--	1,000	--
1988	Pre-Fab Shelters	7,390	3,287	1,650	4,497
1988	Average No. Persons	9.4	8.9	8	7.7
1988	Family Latrines	6,395	2,891	NI	2,785
1988	Sanitation Workers	68	35	12	41
2011	*Shelters*	*8,507*	*2,488*	*1,485*	*5,140*
2011	*Sanitation Workers*	*87*	*30*	*17*	*51*
	Relief				
1988	Feeding Centers mid-day	1	1	1	1
1988	No. Persons Receiving Welfare	4,442	1,448	792	1,690
1988	No. Children Fed	2,350	500	550	1,170
2011	*No. Children Fed*	*UNRWA does not have a feeding programme.*			
2011	*No. of SSN beneficiaries - individuals (cf. people receiving welfare)*	*6,300*	*2,115*	*1,073*	*2,200*
	Health				
1988	Medical Health Centers				
1988	Doctors	5	3	1	4
1988	Dentists	1	PT	PT	PT
1988	Nurses	18	9	5	11
1988	Midwives	--	3	--	4
1988	# Patients Seen Daily	1,110	280	240	NI
2011	*Medical Health Centers*	*2*	*1*	*1*	*1*
2011	*Doctors*	*12*	*5*	*3*	*6*
2011	*Dentists*	*3*	*2*	*1*	*1*
2011	*Nurses*	*14*	*11*	*6*	*13*
2011	*Midwives*	*4*	*2*	*1*	*2*
2011	*No. Patients Seen Daily*	*893*	*414*	*215*	*343*
	Education				
1988	Schools	16	4	4	10
1988	Teachers	331	NI	58	227
1988	Students	14,657	NI	2,291	9,460
1988	Avg Student/Teacher Ratio	44	32	39	42
2011	*Schools*	*16*	*4*	*4*	*10*
2011	*Students*	*15,602*	*2,192*	*2,829*	*9,142*
2011	*Teachers*	*533*	*80*	*88*	*302*
	Community centers				
1988	Youth (6/86)	1	1	1	1
1988	Preschool	4	NI	1	2
1988	Women's Program Centers	1	1	1	1
1988	Rehab Centers	1	1	1	1
2011	*Youth Centers*	*UNRWA no longer has youth centers.*			
2011	*Preschools*	*UNRWA does not have preschools.*			
2011	*Women's Program Centers*	*1*	*1*	*1*	*1*
2011	*Rehab Centers*	*1*	*1*	*1*	*1*

* Number of refugees registered in the camp. NI for No Information

BIBLIOGRAPHY

Below is a partial listing of references used for this book. The number of works on the Middle East, and Palestine in particular, is growing steadily but still does not match the volume of material easily available on Israel. Nor is there much on the camps themselves. Readers who wish to educate themselves further on the subject may refer to the bibliographies in some or all of these books, as many of them are scholarly texts with traditional formats. The author is particularly indebted to those books by Henry Cattan, Sir Geoffrey Furlonge, Ruth Jordan, Dana Adams Schmidt, and Yedida Kalfon Stillman, from whom she has quoted directly or, more often, paraphrased in the preface and epilogue, and in chapters 3, 6, and 12.

Adams, Michael and Christopher Mayhew. *Publish It Not...: The Middle East Cover-Up*. London: Longman, 1975.

Ali, Abdullah Yusuf. Translation of the Qur'an. Mount Holly, NJ: Islamic Educational Service. Third Edition, 1998.

Associated Press. *Lightning Out of Israel: The Six-Day War in the Middle East*. Upper Saddle River, NJ: Prentice Hall, 1967.

Cattan, Henry. *Palestine, the Arabs and Israel: The Search for Justice*. London: Longmans, Green, 1969.

Chacour, Elias. *Blood Brothers*. Grand Rapids, MI: Fleming H. Revell, 1984.

Dekker, Ted and Carl Medearis. *Tea with Hezbollah: Sitting at the Enemies' Table: Our Journey Through the Middle East*. New York: Doubleday Religion, 2010.

Elon, Amos. *The Israelis: Founders and Sons*. London: Weidenfield & Nicholson, 1971.

Fernea, Elizabeth Warnock and Robert A. Fernea. *The Arab World: Personal Encounters*. New York: Anchor Press/Doubleday, 1985.

Findley, Paul. *They Dare to Speak Out*. Connecticut: Lawrence Hill & Company, 1985.

Furlonge, Sir Geoffrey. *Palestine Is My Country: The Story of Musa Alami*. New York: Praeger, 1969.

Goldston, Robert. *The Sword of the Prophet: A History of the Arab World from the Time of Mohammed to the Present Day*. New York: Dial Press, 1979.

Grossman, David. *The Yellow Wind*. New York: Farrar, Strauss & Giroux, 1988.

Halsell, Grace. *Journey to Jerusalem*. New York: Macmillan, 1981.

Hyamson, Albert M. *Palestine Under the Mandate, 1920–1948*. Westport, CT: Greenwood Press, 1976.

Jordan, Ruth. *Daughter of the Waves: Memories of Growing Up in Pre-War Palestine*. New York: Taplinger, 1983.

Kidder, Tracy. *Mountains Beyond Mountains*. New York: Random House, 2003.

Kotner, Norman. *The Earthly Jerusalem*. New York: Charles Scribner's Sons, 1969.

Kramer, Gudrun. *A History of Palestine: From the Ottoman Conquest to the Founding of the State of Israel*. Translated by Graham Harman and Gudrun Krämer. Princeton, NJ: Princeton University Press, 2008. Originally published as Geschichte Palästinas (Munich: Verlag C.H. Beck oHG, 2002).

Love, Kennett. *Suez: The Twice-Fought War*. New York: McGraw-Hill, 1969.

Lowdermilk, Walter. *Palestine: Land of Promise*. New York: Harper & Row, 1944.

Marcus, Amy Dockser. *Jerusalem 1913: The Origins of the Arab-Israeli Conflict*. New York: Viking Penguin, 2007.

Miller, Aaron David. *The Much Too Promised Land: America's Elusive Search for Arab-Israeli Peace*. New York: Bantam Books, 2008.

O'Brien, Conor Cruise. *The Siege: The Saga of Israel and Zionism*. New York: Simon and Schuster, 1986.

Pappe, Ilan. *The Ethnic Cleansing of Palestine*. Oxford, UK: Oneworld Publications Ltd., 2006.

Said, Edward W. *The Question of Palestine*. New York: Random House, 1979.

Schmidt, Dana Adams. *Armageddon in the Middle East: Arab vs. Israeli Through the October War*. The New York Times Survey Series. New York: John Day, 1974.

Soustelle, Jacques. *The Long March of Israel from Theodor Herzl to the Present Day*. New York: American Heritage Press, 1969.

Stillman, Yedida Kalfon. *Palestinian Costume and Jewelry*. Albuquerque, NM: University of New Mexico Press, 1979. © Museum of International Folk Art

Zayid, Ismail. *Zionism: The Myth and the Reality*. Indianapolis, IN: American Trust Publications, 1980.

NOTES

PREFACE

1. An outline, border, or filling stitch. The thread is laid flat on a surface and fastened down with short perpendicular stitches at regular intervals. The embroidery of Ramallah exhibits a greater variety of designs—especially distinctive are its flowers, trees, celestial bodies, animals, and birds, as well as many designs whose beginnings can be traced to medieval Islamic or ancient Near Eastern art. Yedida Kalfon Stillman, *Palestinian Costume and Jewelry* (New Mexico: University of New Mexico Press, 1979), 33.
2. Stillman, *Palestinian Costume and Jewelry*, 32–33.
3. Ibid., 56.

CHAPTER 3

1. Sir Geoffrey Furlonge, *Palestine Is My Country: The Story of Musa Alami* (New York: Praeger, 1969), 155–156.
2. Ibid., 154.
3. Ibid., 155.
4. Ibid., 155–156.
5. Ibid., 156.
6. Ibid., 156.

CHAPTER 6

1. A full description of Abdel-Karim's ordeal can be found in "Israel and Torture," *The London Sunday Times*, June 19, 1977, 17–20.

CHAPTER 7

1. Kennett Love, *Suez: The Twice-Fought War* (New York: McGraw-Hill, 1969), 688–689.
2. Ibid., 690.
3. Henry Cattan, *Palestine, the Arabs and Israel: The Search for Justice*. (London: Longmans, 1969), 132, 235.
4. Kennett Love, *Suez*, 689–690.
5. Henry Cattan, *Palestine, the Arabs and Israel*, 113.
6. Ibid., 107–113.

CHAPTER 13

1. Henry Cattan, *Palestine, the Arabs and Israel: The Search for Justice*. (London: Longmans, 1969), 6.
2. Ibid., 6–7.
3. Ibid., 7.
4. Ruth Jordan, *Daughter of the Waves: Memories of Growing Up in Pre-War Palestine*. (New York: Taplinger, 1983), 31.
5. Ibid., 31–32.
6. Dana Adams Schmidt, *Armageddon in the Middle East: Arab vs. Israeli Through the October War*. *The New York Times* Survey Series. (New York: John Day, 1974), 42.
7. Ibid., 43.
8. Ibid., 43–44.

Made in the USA
Lexington, KY
28 May 2014